50 YEARS
IN THE
BLEACHERS

WHAT MODERN SPORTS PARENTS
CAN LEARN FROM A TITLE IX PIONEER

CHRISTINE HAWKINSON

SILVER STRANDS
PUBLISHING

ISBN: 979-8-9852348-0-0
eBook ISBN: 979-8-9852348-1-7
Library of Congress Control Number: 2021922353

Cover design by Kylee Hawkinson
Cover photo credits:
Chiemi Freund, Shutterstock
onair, Shutterstock
Jason Dent, Unsplash
Dan Thornberg, Shutterstock

Author photos by Paul L. Newby II
Interior design by Damonza

Request special orders from:
Silver Strands Publishing
PO Box 75
Prairie du Sac, WI 53578
or
email *hawkinsonchristine@gmail.com*

SILVER STRANDS
PUBLISHING

Visit the author's website at christinehawkinson.com

Disclaimer: I recognize that others' memories and interpretations of the events described in this book are different than my own and intend no harm to those with differing recollections. I am not a health care professional nor expert in raising human beings. I urge all parents to become informed and use their best judgement when making choices for their children.

To Mom with love and thanks.

You encouraged my love of reading and writing.
You believed in me.
And you taught me that determined women
can create change in the world.

CONTENTS

PREFACE

Long before there was kiddie basketball on Saturday mornings and traveling teams of middle schoolers competing cross-state, when kids practiced alone in their driveways, and more teams were coached by teachers than parents, I had the privilege of learning the game of basketball.

Had I been just four years older, I would have only been an observer of the game I'd watched my father coach. But in the mid-1970s Title IX gave me the opportunity to play, and the experience shaped the woman and sports parent I became.

Twenty years later I was thrilled that my two daughters would have the chance to play much sooner than I had. I hoped they would share my love of basketball and find it as fun and rewarding as I did.

I thought about my high school games and imagined theirs.

Then I got a reality check.

Their game wasn't mine, any more than mine had been my father's.

A lot has changed about youth sports in fifty years. Access, cost, high expectations, and injuries have all become part of the game.

Many parents are overwhelmed by the time and/or money required for their kids to play. Others do not have the means for their children to participate. The Women's Sports Foundation has been working since 1974 to expand access to sports for girls and women. Early in 2022, Under Armour® pledged to break down barriers and create opportunities for more children to play.

Pre-pandemic studies showed that 70% of children were quitting sports before high school. During the pandemic more children dropped out. While cost and access are certainly barriers, there is more to this story.

Many children stop playing because of overbearing coaches, parental pressure, and injuries. Sports should be fun, and for many kids, it is not. If the culture doesn't change, providing more access is not going to keep kids in the game. Introducing sports and skills when age-appropriate, focusing on the purpose of play, and implementing injury prevention programs will.

Navigating the youth sports system is a challenge, and you may be tempted to skip to the end to read my advice or peruse the resources, looking for the magic answer. But storytelling is a process. And as in life, the best lessons will be found along the way. Thank you for joining me in the bleachers.

PROLOGUE

Spring 2002

It was a beautiful sunny morning when the toughest question I'd faced yet as a parent came into our home and wouldn't leave without an answer.

I had started a load of clothes in the washer and was lacing my shoes for a springtime walk when the phone rang. I paced my living room floor with the phone pressed to my ear as I listened to the woman on the other end.

"We are getting some of the girls together for a team and were wondering if you'd let Lauren play in tournaments with them," she said. This was the mother of my daughter's classmate.

"Well, sure. She could play once in a while. We don't want to commit to tournaments every weekend, but in the off-season she could play in a few," I replied, choosing my words carefully. "Will there be practices, too? Who is coaching them?"

"The tournaments aren't every weekend, maybe two or three a month. And they'll only practice once or twice a week."

"Hmm . . . that is a bigger time commitment than we're

able to make. We visit our parents once a month, and since Scott is gone so much as athletic director, we try to do family things when he doesn't have to work on a weekend. She might not be able to make it every time. How many girls are playing? If there are more girls on the team, when families have other obligations, there will still be enough to play."

"Oh. Well, there are only going to be a few girls on the team. We want to keep it small since they all get along and they'll be playing together through high school. They'd really like Lauren to play."

The woman was recruiting next year's seventh-grade girls to be part of a special basketball team, a handpicked subset of the middle school team—what was becoming known as an "elite team," as though naming it as such would make it so.

Elite teams play in tournaments year-round, competing for kids' time and loyalties with school sports teams. Scott and I had agreed that our daughters would play only one sport during each season. And, of course, their school team would always come first.

"I don't think we can commit to that schedule. And we definitely don't want her to play year-round. She's involved in other activities, too."

I was well aware that our decision would create a tough situation for Lauren socially. Middle school girls can be unforgiving. Not participating would change the dynamic between Lauren and her teammates for the next six years. I also knew the elite team would impact the chemistry of the school team, whether Lauren played on the elite team or not.

My stomach rolled. This wasn't how my young daughter's athletics experience was supposed to go. I saw too much wrong with the elite team scenario to ignore what I knew about the sport—and what I knew about my own daughter. I had to stand firm. I was doing the right thing, wasn't I?

My head started to back up my heart. I could hear the voice of my college economics professor. Econ was one of my least favorite classes, but there were two concepts the professor explained that I've applied to many real-life situations. The first: opportunity cost.

"To put it simply, opportunity cost is what you give up to get something else. We often think of opportunity cost in terms of money. The seven dollars you spend on a movie and popcorn can't be used for a new record album. But opportunity cost can also be time and other intangibles. Let's say you plan to study for an exam Thursday night but your friend invites you to go to a movie. Your additional opportunity cost is your study time, and perhaps your grade."

Lauren loved school, read voraciously, and never had to be reminded to practice the piano. The middle school years provide opportunities to try a variety of activities in small doses.

As a sixth grader she'd tried forensics, band, solo/ensemble contest, and the school play. She enjoyed them all and had a circle of friends beyond her basketball teammates. If she played on an elite team, she'd no longer have time for many of the things that were shaping the young woman she was becoming. It wasn't wise for anyone to have their happiness and fulfillment rely on one thing, as I had experienced myself.

If Lauren joined this team, our family would also pay an opportunity cost. In addition to losing valued time together, we'd cut into our discretionary income. Elite teams come with a price tag: unlike a group of kids gathering informally at the park to play ball, elite team tournaments require entry fees, uniforms, gas and hotels, meals, and lots of Gatorade.

I didn't share my financial concerns with the mother I was talking to on the phone, but my worries about the demands on my daughter did not resonate with her. For her daughter, the costs were worth the benefit and participating was the right thing to do. I tried one last time.

"Well, like I said, Lauren could play in tournaments once in a while, but we don't want to commit to something every weekend."

It wasn't the answer she was looking for, and after a few moments of silence she suggested I talk it over with Scott and think about it for a few days. It was clear we were going to have to be all in—or out.

*

I set out for my walk with my heart already pounding. I barely noticed the sunshine and breeze, my mind and body fueled by anger and indignation as my thoughts shifted from our family to the sport I loved. Scott and I had seen a few kids who had played on elite teams for a few years burn out and quit before they reached the varsity level of their school team. We also observed a decline in fundamental skills and knowledge of the game. There was more emphasis on running and shooting than strategy and teamwork. And a growing lack of respect for school coaches and misaligned trust in parent-coaches. Parents less familiar with the game didn't understand why their child was good enough to play all day for a club team but didn't get the same extensive playing time on the school team. What was happening to basketball?

I wanted our daughters to play sports, but not like this. What kind of experience would they have?

I heard my econ professor's voice again as he described the second concept I recalled often, the law of diminishing returns: "You're college students. Let's talk about pizza and beer." He drew on the chalkboard a picture of a pizza cut into eight slices and a pitcher of beer. "Say it's Friday night, and you and your friends go out to celebrate the week being over. You're very hungry and thirsty. Your first slice of pizza and first beer taste great, so you have another of each," he said, crossing off the slice of pizza and glass of beer as they were consumed. "They still both taste pretty good. But you will enjoy each additional slice of pizza and glass of beer less than the previous one. If you keep going, you will eventually experience adverse effects. The tipping point when you begin to feel less, instead of more, enjoyment is the point of diminishing returns."

Those kids who quit in high school had consumed too much. They were not enjoying the game anymore.

For me, this new model for youth sports came with flashing warning lights. Initially some coaches and a few cautious parents voiced concerns, but how do you stop a train gaining momentum? Many parents were buying into the idea that all these changes were good for kids—or they didn't want their own to be left out. It was keeping up with the Joneses, 2000s-style.

On the flip side I thought about the kids this new system left behind. What about the kids whose parents didn't have the financial means or social connections that enabled them to play on an elite team? What about the girls with potential who weren't asked to play because they weren't part of the clique? Why weren't *all* kids given the chance to play?

When Title IX opened the door for my teammates and me to play basketball at Lena-Winslow High School, we all had an equal opportunity. We all had the chance to learn what it meant to be part of a team. A team formed by a common interest and desire to learn. Before we joined the basketball team, some of us barely knew each other, but once the team formed, regardless of age and socio-economic background, we were teammates with a special bond. And we were proud to play for our school. The success we achieved came from our own desire and a coach who provided the structure for learning, not from parents' efforts to orchestrate success.

A couple weeks later the coach of the new seventh-grade elite team called. She told me Lauren *really wanted* to play, and the girls *really wanted* her on the team. She knew I loved the game and was sure that I wanted Lauren to play. The girls were going to have a good team, and Lauren could be part of it. If she didn't participate now, she'd be behind in high school.

I was being asked to ignore my instincts. To ignore what Scott and I knew was happening to youth sports. To ignore my daughter's best interests. But saying no meant my daughter might not find a place on her high school team, playing the game our family loved.

I had first learned the value of sport watching my dad's high school basketball teams play, sharing his enthusiasm for great plays built on solid skills. As a coach's wife I admired the strategy my husband, Scott, applied as he taught his team, choosing an offense and defense to thwart opponents. I loved the game of basketball. I had loved playing. And I wanted to see my daughters play. I wanted them to reap the benefits of playing a sport: to learn about themselves, about teamwork, about strategy.

It is just a game, but this decision would be a defining moment for our daughters and our family. I remember it as clearly as the day I learned I'd have the chance to play.

FUNDAMENTALS

THE PIONEER

Where it began

The bleachers in the Lena-Winslow High School gym were packed for every game, but our family had seats in the top row of the reserved section. Dad had requested them so Mom could have the wall as a backrest, but they also kept my brothers and me corralled. I was nine, Patrick was six, and Daniel was almost four when Dad became the varsity boys' basketball coach. Two years later, baby Michael joined us.

It was the early 1970s and boys' high school sports gave people in our tight-knit northwestern Illinois communities something to look forward to and talk about. Schools provided student fan buses to away games, and many adults, not just parents, religiously drove to rival schools to support their teams. It was way too much work for Mom to take four little kids to an away game, so she'd make popcorn and we'd listen on the radio, but it just wasn't the same as being there.

Oh, how I loved home games. Having only one car, we'd head to the high school with Dad well before game time and leave our coats in the teachers' lounge, a mysterious place where students weren't allowed and where cigarette butts, ink from the mimeograph machine, and empty soda bottles created a bizarre cocktail of scents. Mom would then shepherd us down the hall, into the gym, and up to our perched view of the court.

We would arrive in plenty of time for the warm-ups, which meant we got to enjoy the pep band playing Chicago's "25 or 6 to 4" and themes from TV shows like *Hawaii Five-0* and *Hogan's Heroes*. One of my favorite warm-up songs was "The Horse," an instrumental by Cliff Nobles & Co. that fired up the players and fans, as well as the band. The blare of the horns and thump of the drums stirred anticipation in my chest until the playing of the school song and national anthem signaled we were close to tip-off. As the boys gathered around the bench for the starting lineups, I'd watch Dad give last-minute instructions, reminding them of their assignments based on his scouting report.

From the moment of tip-off, my eyes would be glued to the action. I'd wish the ball into the basket when the score was tight and cross my fingers when our team shot free throws. It took me a while to figure out why players from both teams ran to the opposite end of the court rather than shoot at the nearest basket. But with every game I learned something about the rules and the skills required to play the sport our life revolved around four months of the year. I knew all the boys' names. I began to notice who could shoot from the outside and who would earn Dad's praise for "crashing the boards" or playing "tenacious" defense.

Cued by the halftime buzzer, the smell of popcorn would begin wafting from the cafeteria into the gym, and I'd ask Mom if I could get a Pepsi. The hot gym made me thirsty, and this was my chance to be independent and get away from my brothers, if only for a few minutes. She'd nod, holding Michael on her slender hip, standing between Pat and Dan to keep the peace as she swayed and hummed along with the band's rendition of her favorite song, "Sweet Caroline."

I'd then hurry to the cafeteria where the air was thick with cigarette smoke and coaching critiques. Men nodded and smiled at me mid-sentence; I was too young to understand that, depending on the night, the discussion may have been about whether my father should stay or go as head coach.

I'd quickly drink my Pepsi, drawn from a portable fountain and served in a four-ounce paper cup, then head back to my seat to watch the pom-pom girls. I loved the band but looked forward to the day I could participate in the excitement by dancing with the pom-pom girls. After their performance, the boys would return to the court and we would settle in for the second half, cheering for the Panthers, win or lose.

After the game we'd wait impatiently for Dad to finish his duties and see the last boy off for the night. Once home, Dad would let me look at the scorebook. I loved how the neatly written twos and circles with an "x" through them added up perfectly across columns and down rows to tell the game's story.

By the time I was in eighth grade, I knew the game better than most boys my age. But there was no reason to dream of playing.

Thank you, Bernice Sandler*

By the end of Dad's fifth season as head coach, he and Mom had a well-established routine for the off-season. As was often the case before supper, Dad was drinking a martini in the kitchen, still in the dress pants and wingtip shoes he wore for his job as our junior high principal, his clip tie off and top shirt button unbuttoned. He leaned against the counter and talked to Mom as she kept watch over several pots on the stove, her clothing protected by the half-apron that was once her mother's. Johnny Cash and June Carter sang from the living room stereo. I emerged from my bedroom where I had been doing homework before Mom called me to set the table. I demonstrated my dislike for the task by tossing the plates onto the table. Maybe it wasn't the task I disliked so much as the fact that my brothers were never asked to do it. It was 1975; I'd heard of women's liberation, after all.

I expected to hear one of Dad's recurring themes: reinventing the wheel in education, teachers who lacked classroom discipline, or a student who just didn't get it and needed a swift kick in the rear. Instead, he turned to me as I plunked the last plate on the table.

"Christine, I have some exciting news! Have you ever heard of Title IX? It refers to some legislation passed in '72. Part of it says we have to offer an equal number of sports to both girls and boys. Our boys have football, basketball, and track, but girls only have volleyball and track. It sounds like we'll probably start a girls' basketball team next year when you're in high school."

Instead of heading back to my bedroom until dinner, I started asking questions, most of which wouldn't be answered for months. Who would coach us? When would we start? How many girls did Dad think would want to play? And the big question I voiced only to myself, "Will I be good enough to make the team?"

Adding the sport would complicate the scheduling of

games and practices in our district's limited gym space and directly affect the varsity boys' basketball team he coached, but Dad never questioned that girls should have the opportunity. He knew the kids in our small school district well and began naming potential players and how they could apply their athleticism and work ethic to basketball.

That night after supper I spent the first of many evenings shooting baskets in the driveway. My plans to be a pom-pom girl faded as the universe offered another option. Basketball was the only sport I liked enough to consider playing, but I had a lot to learn. And I had more on my mind than learning the game. Could a basketball player emerge from the cocoon of a quiet bookworm? Would playing earn me respect or disdain from my classmates? Would I make Dad proud or embarrass him?

It never occurred to me that I was about to become a pioneer—one of thousands of young women who would pave the way for our daughters to play sports, pursue male-dominated careers, and make the most of their abilities.

No person in the United States shall, on the basis of sex, be excluded from participation in, be denied the benefits of, or be subjected to discrimination under any education program or activity receiving Federal financial assistance.
—TITLE IX OF THE EDUCATION AMENDMENTS OF 1972

* Bernice Sandler, known as the "Godmother of Title IX," was a college professor instrumental in the passage of Title IX.

Blazing the trail

My first day of high school happened to fall on my fourteenth birthday. After three years of walking down the east side of Fremont Street to the junior high, I switched to the west sidewalk that led to the high school situated directly across the street. The street that separated two very different worlds. The high school was older and darker, and the halls were filled with upperclassman, who mostly ignored but were rumored to torment freshmen.

By October I settled into a routine. Classes were harder, but that was to be expected. It was tough for me to embrace geometry, but I loved French class, where I learned something new every day. On Friday nights I joined my friends at the football games where we'd talk nonstop as we walked loops around the field and occasionally checked the score.

One morning before school started, as my friends and I gathered in the freshman hallway laughing about the TV shows we'd watched the night before, three junior girls approached us with a clipboard.

"We have a petition to start a girls' basketball team. Do any of you want to play?" Paula asked.

A petition! I thought Dad had said we'd likely have a team. If the school board was reconsidering, we had to let them know we wanted it. In the months since Dad told me about Title IX, I'd been practicing in the driveway and finding the courage to play in front of an audience. I was both intimidated and excited about this opportunity. I nodded and added my signature. Paula smiled approvingly, and my stomach flipped. Paula Miller was asking me to join her team.

Dad had told us stories at the dinner table about Paula

Miller. She grew up playing basketball with the boys in Winslow, and everyone knew she was better than most of them. Paula excelled in track, volleyball, and every other sport she played. She and her friends scared the hell out of me. But here they were, talking to us!

I'm going to play with Paula Miller?! Who will coach us? Are we really going to have a team? I felt rebellious signing the petition—taking my own stand for women's lib—and forged an immediate alliance with the other girls who pledged their interest. By afternoon I wondered if my signing would cause a problem for Dad. And I was scared. This was a far cry from shooting in the driveway. But there was no turning back. I definitely wanted to play.

With the Title IX requirement to provide an equal number of sports for girls and boys, our team probably would have started without the petition, but it was empowering to believe we had influenced the decision. Late in the fall of 1975, an announcement and a sign-up sheet appeared in the girls' locker room, along with a practice schedule. While a handful of the girls who played volleyball or led cheers came out for the team, basketball attracted many girls who didn't play other sports. Girls from varied economic backgrounds. Girls who knew each other but didn't hang out as friends. Girls who had no experience with the game but were willing to learn.

Marvin Kaiser was the brave man who was going to coach us. Mr. Kaiser was one of our high school gym teachers. Up until the 1990s coaches were always teachers in the school district. They knew the kids and they knew the school rules. The court or field was an extension of the classroom and expectations were similar. Players and parents may not have always agreed with coaches and some complained, but ultimately everyone understood the coach was in charge of the team. Most parents knew that it was typical for teenagers to complain about practice or the coach, and they reminded their children to respect the coach, listen, and learn.

Mr. Kaiser easily commanded our respect. "On the line!" his deep voice boomed from his well-over-six-foot-tall body, and it didn't take long for us to stop shooting and stand attentively on the end line as he started practice. Most of his players didn't know the rules of the game or have any fundamental skills. He had no choice but to begin with the basics.

The first couple of weeks we learned how to dribble, first in place, then moving across the court at varied speeds, learning to feel the ball rather than watch it. We practiced the correct way to send a chest pass, bounce pass, and overhead pass to our teammates. We learned the difference between a layup, set shot, and jump shot. We shuffled our feet in defensive position, making large figure eights around the court until our quadriceps burned. Mr. Kaiser inserted a smaller metal rim inside one of the baskets so he could shoot without the ball going in as he taught us how to block out and rebound.

We only had a few weeks to prepare for our first game, so he had to move quickly into teaching us strategy. He blew his whistle and we gathered around him.

"Tonight we're going to learn our offense," Mr. Kaiser announced.

Eager to learn how to play more than 21 and HORSE, I listened intently.

"We are going to play a 1-3-1 offense. Bert is our point guard. She is the "one" at the top of the circle. Then he directed

Beth and Amy to the left and right wing positions and put Louise in the middle to form the "three." Ruth took the "one" spot under the basket. Then Mr. Kaiser directed Bert to pass the ball to Amy on the right wing, and Amy to pass it back as Bert cut to the basket for a layup.

We watched them a few times, then they ran the same play on the left side of the basket. When Mr. Kaiser had a defensive player step in to stop Bert, Amy could get a pass to Louise in the center instead. He added layers one by one so we could see all the variations of what had seemed simple in the beginning. We learned the correct way to set a pick on the defense. If we stood behind and slightly to the side of the defender, our teammate could dribble by us both to get an open shot, and we could beat her defender to the basket for the rebound.

For that first year we stuck to the 1-3-1 offense. And for defense: man-to-man. *Girl-to-girl,* we joked. In neighboring Iowa, high school girls' teams had six players on the court. Three would play defense, and three would be on offense, with players passing the ball from one end of the court to their team- mates on the other end. In Illinois, girls were going to play with five on the court just like the boys, and we learned it was just as important to play good defense as it was to score.

Throughout our practices Mr. Kaiser drilled some cardinal rules into our heads:

"Never give up the base line!"

"Never let the opponent push you under the basket."

"Move your feet! Don't be caught standing still!"

The week before our first game Mr. Kaiser taught us new rules or protocols every night. We learned how to arrange our- selves on the circle for a jump ball. This was long before the possession arrow was implemented, so jump balls happened many times during each game and on different areas of the court. We had a different play depending on whether we were in the middle of the court or on one of the free throw circles.

We learned about the restraining line, and the three-, five-, and ten-second rules. We learned how to report into the game at the scorer's desk and to relay the number of the player we were guarding to our replacement when we came out of the game.

Mr. Kaiser, addressing my friend Beth, explained how to line up for free throws: "Beth, you're the shooter. The defense gets the two inside spots near the basket. Then the shooter's teammates get the next two. The next two spots are for two more defenders, with the last defender out top behind the shooter, ready for a fast break. I want a guard from the shooter's team back there to be ready on defense."

Finally, after four weeks of learning these fundamentals, we were ready to scrimmage. He assigned us to teams, one wearing red pinnys, the other blue. "Mr. Kaiser? My pinny is blue. Am I on defense or offense?" someone asked, not understanding that she'd be playing both during a game.

The man had a lot of patience. I think he genuinely enjoyed the challenge of teaching us the game. As he got to know us, he would tease, joke, and laugh, and we knew he really cared about us as individuals. He probably didn't think about the fact that he, too, was making history. Though I'm sure he realized, far more than we did, just how big the gap was between the girls' and boys' game.

*

Because the boys' basketball games had been scheduled a year or two in advance, adding girls' basketball created scheduling and facility challenges. Our practices were scheduled around the established boys' times, usually in the evening and in the junior high gym. After school I would walk home, do my homework, and eat supper. Then I'd pack my duffel bag, bundle back up, and cut through the backyards to the street. On bright winter nights moonlight on the snow lit the path to the railroad tracks on my half-mile trek back to school. I took that walk so many times that even forty-five years later, on crisp winter evenings, I still hear basketballs hitting the hardcourt.

If the boys had an away game, we got to practice in the high school gym after school the night before our games. The boys' teams always got the preferred gyms and time slots in those early years.

My duffel bag contained my practice gear: cut-off denim jeans, an old t-shirt, two pairs (to prevent blisters) of knee-high tube socks with black and gold stripes at the top, and Pro Ked black canvas sneakers. At least choosing our own clothes differentiated the basketball team from gym class, where we wore the much-maligned 1970s baby blue one-piece gym suit with short sleeves and elastic legs. The boys had practice uniforms long before the girls got them.

The boys also had comfortable uniforms to play in. We inherited the volleyball team's old uniforms, and the following year new ones were purchased for varsity girls' basketball—black for away games, white for home. The shorts were snug and see-through, and more than one of us was embarrassed to realize we'd worn patterned or colored underwear on game day. To make matters worse, they were extremely short, so we spent as much time tugging our shorts down over our rears as we did tucking our bra straps into the sleeveless top. Though sports bras began to be commercially available in the late 1970s, none of us were lucky enough to own one. Not much thought had yet gone into what would be comfortable for girls playing basketball. Though they are poked fun at today, at least the boys' short basketball shorts and tank style tops allowed them to move without restriction.

There were many inequities, but at the time we didn't really notice. We were just happy to play basketball.

My first game
"Is the team ready, Chris?"

Our geometry teacher had followed our progress and, like other curious teachers, students, and community members, planned to attend our first game.

"Yes, we're excited about a real game," I replied. *And scared to death.* I barely heard what he said that day about calculating the degrees of an angle. I tried to calm the somersaults my stomach was turning. *I probably won't even get in the game. I'm just going to sit on the bench and watch.*

The hour hand of the school clocks moved faster than normal that day. My adrenaline rushed as I walked home from school and did my homework. I wasn't hungry and barely tasted the sandwich Mom made me. I knew I needed to eat something, but not too much. *A hungry dog runs faster.* I triple-checked the contents of my duffel bag to be sure I wasn't forgetting something and headed back to school. I breathed in the winter air, my footsteps echoing on the pavement under the moon.

My teammates and I dressed quietly. Our manager, Julie,

let Mr. Kaiser know when we were ready for him to come into the locker room for our pregame talk. We sat silently on the benches. He scanned our faces and laughed a little. "Are you girls okay?"

"Mr. Kaiser, how many people are out there?"

"What if we forget what we're supposed to do?"

"How many seconds do we get to throw the ball in?"

"Whoa . . . calm down. Everything's going to be all right. Just do what we've worked on in practice. I'll call time-out if we need to review anything. You're going to be fine. Remember what we've been working on. Just like we practiced girls, just like practice."

We ran out of the locker room and began our warm-up drills. The varsity girls were there to watch us, as were some of our parents and a few community members. More would arrive in time for the varsity game. Mom, Dad, and my youngest brother, Michael, were sitting on the top row of the bleachers. Brothers Pat and Dan were somewhere in the student section with their friends.

I watched as the sophomores started the game. The other team was just as nervous as we were; players on both teams traveled, carried the ball, and had to be reminded how to line up on the free throw lane. Just as I started to relax a little, Beth elbowed me and said, "Chris, Mr. Kaiser wants you."

I moved up the bench to sit next to him. He put his hand on my shoulder and said, "I want you to go in for Bert. Louise is going to take the ball out, and I want you to bring it up and run the plays—just like we did in practice."

I nodded and went to the scorer's bench to check in as he'd taught us. On the next dead ball, the referee waved me in, and as I stood near half court watching my opponent shoot a free throw, I could feel my kneecaps shaking.

I don't recall if we won the game, and I'd like to think I didn't play any worse than anyone else, but my individual game statistics give an indication of the quality of play. I had thirteen turnovers, including seven bad passes; I missed four free throws and only made one of four field goal attempts; and I had three fouls. I did, however, steal the ball once and win one jump ball.

Once I had that first game under my belt, I couldn't wait for the next one, and the one after that. I'm happy to say that I never again made so many turnovers in one game. On defense, I challenged myself every time down the court to stay between my player and the basket and stop her from scoring. I played away from the basket and wasn't very tall so snaring a rebound by blocking out taller girls was a little victory. Causing a turnover or missing a shot strengthened my intention to get it right the next time down the court. Slowly, my skills grew. So did my confidence.

I began to understand the power of teamwork. The satisfaction of sending a precise pass to my teammate so she could score. The positive energy generated when we all played good defense and stopped the other team from scoring. The encouragement we gave each other to keep trying when things weren't going well.

Most importantly, I was having fun. I looked forward to every practice, every game.

Though some people saw girls' sports and women's lib as an "invasion," Title IX had provided a place for me to expand how I thought about myself and what I could do in the future. Playing basketball was an unexpected opportunity I knew was worth the potential ridicule. I'd been a careful observer of the game for the last five years, watching Dad coach the varsity boys. I wanted some of what they had. When our six-game first season ended, I counted down the weeks on the calendar until our second season would begin. I had work to do.

THE COACH'S DAUGHTER

Lessons on the driveway

"Pass me the ball!" Dad ordered as he stepped out of the house onto the top of three steps leading to the driveway. He was a good thirty feet from the basket as he launched the ball toward the hoop yelling, "Bato!"

"Christine, did I ever tell you about Bato?" he asked for the hundredth time. "He was a senior when I was in eighth grade. He was an incredible shooter, averaged about twenty-five points a game. He was probably the best ball player in Chicago at that time. But Ray Meyer at DePaul was the only one who showed interest in him until he was MVP of the North/South all-star game. That raised the interest of University of Illinois, but Bato chose DePaul because Ray Meyer was interested in him from the beginning.

"Practice shooting every day, and you might be almost as good as Bato."

I didn't think I'd ever be as good as Dad's hero, Bato, but when we learned I would actually get to play on a high school team, I got serious about shooting the basketball correctly.

Previously, I used the backboard to get my shots to fall, with pretty good success. But that wouldn't do in a real game. Dad taught me the correct way to shoot.

"Put your fingers on the seam, bring the ball up in front of your face, keep your elbow in, and aim four inches above the rim. Bend your knees. Release the ball as you come up. Follow through, reaching for the rim, then follow your shot," he instructed me.

I struggled at first to change my habit. Most of my shots missed their mark. Then, as the weeks passed, I learned to pay more attention to my feet, my knees, squaring my body to the basket, the angle of my shooting arm, my elbow, my fingers on the seams of the ball, the release, the spin, the follow through, tuning into each aspect of my shot until muscle memory took over and I could recognize exactly what I'd done wrong when the ball clunked off the rim.

Mom and Dad spent those summer evenings relaxing in lawn chairs, sitting in the yard near the driveway. Mom watched quietly as Dad continued to tell stories. I practiced shooting or dribbling figure eights around my legs. Dad showed me several drills to make it more interesting, like the Mikan Drill.

"Start under the basket. Now step with your left foot and make a right-handed layup. Get your rebound and go off your right foot to make a left-handed layup. Get your rebound and go right again. See how many you can make in thirty seconds."

The drill challenged my ball-handling and footwork, to say nothing of my patience. But I was determined to get it right, and it became part of my practice routine.

"George Mikan never played basketball in high school," said Dad. "He was almost seven feet tall. Ray Meyer discovered him and taught him the game. He made him shoot right- and left-handed hook shots with a towel under his other arm so he could learn proper form. He later played in the NBA and was one of the best ball players ever."

In addition to history lessons, Dad offered random words of wisdom.

"Never eat too much before a game. A hungry dog runs faster."

"You can dribble too much, and you can shoot too much, but you can never rebound too much."

His comments were never punitive, but he did call me out when I got lazy.

"Keep your elbow in, Christine."

"Follow through. Pretend you're going to grab the rim."

I began to find peace in the rhythm of dribbling and the discipline of daily practice. I took the same shots over and over and over. I found a couple sweet spots on the court where I rarely missed. Some days the blacktop, hoop, basketball, and I aligned like stars in a galaxy. I knew the moment the ball left my hand that it was going to swish through the net. I was unwittingly learning the power of discipline and persistence.

One evening, everything I put up went in. Every time the ball left my fingertips, I knew it was on target. Shot after shot, the methodic swish of the hoop confirmed I was a basketball player. It felt great, and I couldn't help but smile. Dad rose slowly from his chair.

"Christine, you're getting cocky. I need to beat you in a game of HORSE."

Dad didn't tolerate egos on his team and certainly not from his children. But that didn't stop his own. As I missed the shot that gave me an "E," he advised me, "Christine, wherever you go, and whatever you do, remember the honor of Lane!"

Then he celebrated his win by singing the student-version of his high school fight song:

Go, Lane, we're with you,
Go, Lane, we'll cheer you,
Go, Lane, and win this game.
Just take this as a little tip,
The other team is full of shit.
So go, Lane, go, Lane, go!
We'll win if you
Go, Lane, go Lane, go!

Dirt courts and metal rims

When Mom and Dad had our house built in 1971, the driveway was gravel. Later, when they were ready to replace the gravel with blacktop, Dad made sure there was an area to put up a basketball hoop with room to shoot from fifteen to twenty feet away all the way around. It was a luxury he couldn't have imagined as a kid growing up in his neighborhood melting pot near Wrigley Field.

My dad, Richard "Dick" Maher, grew up in Chicago in the 1930–40s. He and his childhood friends with German, Irish, or Polish last names played hide-and-go-seek in a neighborhood block, or dodgeball or baseball in the street, using cars as bases. Older kids looked out for the younger ones. One day, a couple high school boys extended an invitation that changed Dad's life. They asked him to a basketball game. The sixth grader had never been to a high school game and was glad to tag along. They rode the streetcar to Evanston where they saw St. George play De La Salle.

"That night I saw my first basketball game and a ball player named Joe Apple. He played left wing and had a very nice two-handed set shot. I couldn't understand how he could put that ball up in the air and make it go in the basket," Dad recalled. "After school the next day, I ran home, put on my old clothes, and rode my bike to Brands Park. It was early winter and cold. I checked out a basketball from the park district office. The basketball court was dirt. The rims on the metal backboards had no nets. And I went home for supper very disappointed. I was zero for 999 because I didn't know how to shoot!"

Dad went back to the park over the next few days to practice. Some high school boys saw him struggling, and they taught him how to shoot the ball. When summer rolled around, there were full-court games that went on all day long. Boys got in line and waited for their turn to play. Winners stayed on the court; losers went to the end of the line. That was how Dad learned to play the game. As an eighth grader, he was the youngest player on a factory-sponsored team in the park league, and they won a trophy. He headed to high school with hopes of making the team.

Remember the honor of Lane

Go, Lane, go
Go, Lane
For we are here to cheer for you,
Go, Lane
To you we'll e'er be true.
Be fearless and bold for the Myrtle and the Gold,
Add laurels to our fame
(Go, Lane, go)

Go, Lane, we're with you,
Go, Lane, we'll cheer you,
Go, Lane, and win this game;
Just take this as a little tip,
We're bound to win the championship,
So go, Lane, go, Lane, go!
(We're with you!)
Go, Lane, go Lane, go!

(Hit 'em high! Hit 'em low!)
Go, Lane, go!
Go, Lane

—WRITTEN BY JACK T. NELSON,
CLASS OF 1915

In the fall of 1947, Dad enrolled at Lane Technical High School. Around five thousand students from a variety of ethnic backgrounds attended the all-boys school.

During the first week of school, Dad, and a couple hundred other freshmen, tried out for Coach Ray Umbright's last period physical education class. Though technically the last class of the day, it consisted entirely of basketball players and was essentially the beginning of basketball practice, and continued when the school day ended. My dad was the first one picked. In following years there were no try-outs; rather boys learned that they were still on the team when their fall class schedule indicated they had PE class with Coach Umbright last period.

Lane Tech had two teams, the junior team and the senior team. The juniors couldn't be taller than five feet seven inches. Being five feet nine inches, Dad played with the seniors, who could be any height.

"We played man-to-man and various zone defenses. On offense we played with two guards out front. One would pass to the forward on his side, run around him to the baseline, and receive a return pass for the shot. We called it 'guard around.' Against a zone we passed the ball around quickly, and whoever got an open shot took it. It was not sophisticated basketball. One time we had to play Marshall High School. They were coached by one of the first Chicago area coaches who attended clinics. They played a full-court diamond press. We had no idea what that was, and they ran away with the ball game."

Coach Umbright's team came from diverse backgrounds, from low to middle income families. The school provided uniforms, and they all wore white canvas Chuck Taylor Converse shoes. Egos weren't tolerated, everyone was accepted on equal footing.

Every morning Dad walked or hitchhiked one mile to school. Basketball games were played right after school, and the boys walked or took streetcars to get to the opponent's gym. There were no prepacked sandwiches or concession stands, so their pregame meal was whatever they had for lunch, and they didn't eat again until they got home that night. After the game they went their separate ways, walking or taking the streetcar to their own neighborhood. There were seldom, if ever, parents at the games. Grandma never saw her son play; Grandpa saw him play once.

Throughout high school most of the guys wanted or needed a job to help their family when basketball season ended. Lane Tech had an employment office that connected students with small businesses, factories, or even individuals who needed workers. One year Dad worked for a guy who owned a sailboat. His job was to get the boat ready for summer by doing basic maintenance. He also worked for a while at a distribution warehouse, filling orders for a couple hours after school.

But when he wasn't working, he played basketball. On Saturdays Grandma packed him a lunch, and he took the streetcar to Hamlin Park where there was an indoor gym with a little balcony above one of the backboards. Boys wanting to play got in line, forming teams in groups of five. Winners stayed on the court to take on the next challengers. Dad met and played with boys from other schools and neighborhoods until he graduated from Lane Tech in 1951.

Decades later Dad said, "Because of basketball, I finished high school. In the late 1940s it was quite popular to quit school at sixteen and work in a factory to make money for a car and cigarettes. Because of basketball I got a high school education, enjoyed my military service, and met your mother. Without the game of basketball, I don't know what the hell would have happened to me, and that's why I'll have a picture of a basketball on my tombstone. Not because I was a great player—I wasn't—but because the game did so much for me in life."

Of the hundreds in his freshman class who had tried out for the team, Dad and four of his teammates played four years of basketball for Lane Tech. Many lifelong friendships were forged. Throughout their lives, and well into their 80s, Dad and his teammate Ron Nikcevich visited on the telephone regularly. Ron's family was Serbian and lived about five miles from Lane Tech in the opposite direction from Dad's house. Had it not been for basketball, they never would have met. Dad had no reason to suspect that one day his only daughter would also be part of a unique group of basketball players.

A coach is born

The paragraph next to Dad's senior photo in the Lane Tech High School yearbook says he was "undecided" about his future plans. He spent the summer after high school graduation in eastern Pennsylvania with his mother and her family. The night they returned to Chicago, he found his friends at a bar near Brands Park, the same park where he'd learned to shoot a basketball. They were joining the service the next morning and asked if he wanted to enlist with them. He went home to pack and told his parents he was leaving in the morning.

After completing basic training, when he wasn't attending classes or fulfilling duties, he shot baskets in the base gym and played on his base basketball teams. They traveled by train or plane to play other bases and small colleges, with the intent of boosting morale. Those games did that and more for Dad. After spraining his ankle during one contest, he offered to coach his team against one of their biggest rivals.

When Dad returned to Chicago in 1955, after four years in the Air Force, he was no longer undecided about his future. He contacted his high school friend and teammate Ron Nikcevich, who could only laugh when Dad called him out of the blue asking him to meet him at the train station in Macomb.

Ron was a senior on the Western Illinois State Teachers College (now Western Illinois University) basketball team with plans to be an English teacher after graduation. Dad claimed that within thirty minutes of arriving on campus, Ron helped him get registered for classes and introduced him to Coach LeRoy "Stix" Morley, who welcomed him to the basketball team. Dad moved into Barracks Three, one of the makeshift housing units the college had added to accommodate enrollment boosted by veterans.

When he wasn't in class or at practice, Dad played pickup basketball games in Morgan Gym, where a pretty young woman would often be playing the organ in the hallway. He and his buddies would often take breaks and do their best to distract her.

Dad asked her out and they dated through the spring term, but the young woman had been persuaded by her best friend from high school to transfer to St. Louis University for her junior year. Dad was sorry to see her transfer, and then he faced another disappointment midway through his sophomore year of college.

"There were a lot of gifted basketball players on the team. Ron was the sixth man and made Second Team All-Conference. The coach had eight or nine guys who could be starters, including Chuck Schramm, who was drafted by the Boston Celtics and made it to the last cut before the season started. After the final practice week of my second year, we had the inter-squad scrimmage, and I knew the competition was more than I could play with. I scored a total of two points in my college career."

He was done playing, but he had enjoyed coaching in the Air Force and decided to apply his love of the game to coaching kids once he earned his teaching degree. He worked at a gas station and washed dishes at a retirement home while he finished college.

*

One time Dad traveled to St. Louis for a Cardinals game, and he tried to get in touch with the young woman who had transferred to St. Louis University, but she had gone home for the Mother's Day weekend. She was surprised to find a note that he'd called while she was gone. After graduating, she took a teaching job near Saint Louis, and the following December, when Dad graduated from Western, he moved to Saint Louis and took substitute teaching jobs. My parents resumed dating, soon set a wedding date, and decided to move to the Chicago area where there was a huge demand for teachers in the suburbs.

When Dad interviewed for a job in the Palatine School District, he got an offer, and they offered a job to Mom as well, without even meeting her. They both worked for junior high schools in the district. Dad taught PE and coached track and basketball; Mom taught Social Studies and English until she resigned just before I was born.

Dad coached for five years, and Mom attended fewer of

his games as our family grew. Patrick was born three years after me, and Daniel almost three years after that. In addition to coaching, Dad became the PE curriculum director for the Arlington Heights elementary school district, and he spent three years going to night school, earning his master's degree in school administration at Roosevelt University. He arrived home after midnight two or three times a week from his classes in North Chicago.

In his absence Mom became a full-time mother, household manager, and supportive wife. Like all coach's spouses, most parenting fell to her during the season. Dad couldn't have done his job without her support. And his teams became an extension of our family and our lives during the season.

Winslow, Illinois, population 350

My journey would have been much different had my parents not chosen to leave the Chicago suburbs when I was nine. Life there seemed fine to me, especially in the summer. I climbed the apple trees in our backyard, played hopscotch on the sidewalk with the neighbor girls, and sat at my bedroom window, playing school or writing poems at the old wooden school desk with the slanted lift-top that Dad had saved from the dumpster. If the Cubs were playing, I'd watch the game with Dad, keeping track of Ron Santos's and Ernie Banks's achievements on my handwritten roster. Other times we sat on the patio and listened to Jack Brickhouse give the play-by-play on WGN radio.

Airplanes passed overhead throughout the day on their way to or from O'Hare, and the expressway was just a few miles from our home. I was oblivious to the civil unrest and the 1968 riots in Chicago, but I knew Dad was concerned about drugs and people he called hippies. Though he'd grown up in Chicago, he and Mom began looking for a different place to raise their family.

Now armed with a master's degree, Dad had several interviews around the state before he was offered the junior high principal position at the consolidated school district of Lena-Winslow in northwestern Illinois. When the school board learned he coached basketball, they also offered him the varsity job. In August of 1970, just before my ninth birthday, our family left the Chicago area. Observing my parents approach this new adventure with openness and enthusiasm greatly influenced how I've approached change throughout my life.

None of the few homes for sale in Lena met our needs, so we lived in Winslow for one year while a house was built on an open lot in an established neighborhood near the cemetery. We rented a red brick Victorian home. Pat, Dan, and I explored every nook and cranny of that big old house. In those days, elementary-aged kids were not directed how and when to play. We made discoveries and used our imagination every day. The three of us shared the back bedroom that spanned the width of the second floor. I set up my Barbie dolls' make-believe life in the walk-in bedroom closet and spent many hours in the guest room at the front of the house, seated at the window reading books, writing poems, or taking pretend restaurant orders.

My brothers and I fought over the swing that hung on the front porch where we gathered in the evening to watch the cars pass by. The homeowners had two ponies that lived in the old barn at the end of the backyard, and if we were lucky enough to be outside when they came to feed them, we'd get a ride. Sometimes, in the evening, our family would walk to the center of town to get a drink of cold fresh water from the artesian well.

On his ten-mile commute to Lena, driving south on Highway 73 flanked by cornfields and milking barns, Dad would laugh as he listened to the Chicago traffic report and wonder what his high school buddies would say. People learned quickly that we were the family of the new junior high principal and varsity basketball coach, and having grown up in Chicago, Dad was baffled by how friendly everyone was, but he thoroughly enjoyed it.

Dad used to buy eggs at a farm. I would chase gray kittens in the barn while he chatted with the farmer. One evening Dad took us to a livestock auction just to see what it was all about. I watched quietly from the tiered seating in the round barn as animals were brought to the circle of dirt in the middle for showing. I tried to understand what was happening. When I complained about the smell, Dad laughed and said, "Christine, you'd better get used to it. You'll probably marry a farmer some day!"

Like my parents, I embraced our small town, as it allowed me a new independence. When I memorized the combination that unlocked the bronze-colored door on our mailbox, I was deemed old enough to walk or ride my bike the two blocks to the post office alone. When school started, I would walk Patrick to our new school where he attended first grade and I fourth.

Since we only had one car, Mom was grateful most everything we needed could be found "downtown." She could walk to the grocery store with Dan and pull our meals home in a wagon. There was also a doctor's office, a restaurant, and a bank. And of course, the barber shop, where Dad furthered his education in rural living, starting with his first visit for a haircut.

The farmer in the chair glanced up. The owner, Ron, kept the razor moving and nodded as Dad came through the door.

"You're the new basketball coach?" Ron asked.

"Yes, I am."

"Where are you from?" Ron asked.

"Chicago"

"Coached before?"

"Yes. Junior high for seven years."

"Are you a magician?"

"No," Dad laughed.

"Well, you'd better be if you want to be a winner down there."

He kindly filled Dad in on the history of Le-Win basketball, which hadn't seen a lot of success. And on the school district, which had had no financial choice but to consolidate twelve years earlier. The merger was still a sore spot for some of the folks in Winslow as their former high school was now the elementary school Pat and I attended. Junior and senior high school students in Winslow were bused to Lena, along with kids from the even smaller towns in our district: McConnell, Elroy, and Waddams Grove. Dad's basketball team would be comprised of boys who had grown up in each of the towns, too far apart to have played at the park together while growing up like he had with boys in his neighborhood.

School sports provided the opportunity to unite the boys—and our communities—as they competed against the other small-town schools in our conference. Dad embraced his new challenge. He was eager to begin coaching. He liked to win, but even before talking to Ron, he knew he'd have to sell the boys on his magic.

Get with the program

On the first day of practice, Dad introduced himself and told the boys a few stories about his previous coaching experience. Then he shared his philosophy about high school sports and the basketball program he was going to run. The boys listened politely, waiting to hear something they could relate to. Confused, one of the boys finally raised his hand.

"Coach, what's this program you keep talking about?"

Dad's program encompassed his coaching philosophy, behavioral expectations of his team on and off the court, drills, and plays. Lots and lots of plays. Each boy received a booklet titled *Plays and Patterns* that Dad had written by hand and copied on the school's mimeograph machine for each player. Outlined in faint purple ink on the cover was the school mascot, Perky the Panther, standing on a large basketball labeled "Le-Win Basketball" and a handwritten speech balloon from Perky saying, "*You can never rebound too much!*"

The booklet described Dad's plays for what he called his "regular" offense, the 1-3-1, with adjustments against a zone defense. He'd drawn out offenses to play against a man-to-man defense or a full-court zone press, which came with the added warning, "DO NOT DRIBBLE!" and the encouragement, "Playing against the press is fun!" There were plays for fast breaks, plays for stalling, plays for trapping the ball on defense. The hand-drawn basketball courts with arrows and numbers corresponded to numbered steps alongside. Some of them came with added directions like this:

You Must

1. Play without the ball
2. Fake (hard cuts)
3. Pivot
4. Pass (<u>bounce</u>)
5. Dribble (correct hand)
6. React. <u>THINK!</u>

And Dad's expectation about his playbook was clearly stated at the top of the first page:

KNOW WHAT THESE ARE BEFORE NOV. 9th
ASK QUESTIONS AT PRACTICE
STUDY YOUR HANDOUT <u>AT HOME</u> – <u>NOT</u>
IN <u>SCHOOL</u>!

I'd hazard a guess that most of the boys were not inclined to do basketball homework, but they learned quickly that their coach, who planned his practices down to the minute, did indeed expect them to learn the plays.

Dad's program was a belief system paired with strategy. Everything he said and did was with a purpose, right down to ordering Chuck Taylor Converse shoes for all the boys so they looked, as well as played, like a team.

Day by day, practice by practice, as the boys saw Dad's ideas successfully executed, they began to buy into them. Their respect for him grew, as his did for them.

He often marveled at how their lives differed from his at their age. Most of the boys lived on farms and were expected to milk cows and do other farm chores before school and between practices and games. Two of his first-string players drove the garbage truck and picked up our trash on Saturday mornings. Many of them liked to hunt—something Dad knew nothing about— and he lost ground with them when he scheduled practice on the first day of deer hunting season. After the boys barely spoke to him during that morning practice, Dad's breakfast companions at the local eatery explained the seriousness of his mistake.

He pleaded ignorance and made a sincere apology to the boys. They responded by working harder on the fundamentals their coach insisted were so important.

In Dad's coaching debut the Panthers handed an unexpected loss to conference favorite, Orangeville. His point guard told him, "We kind of thought you'd like to win your first game here." The team did more than win their first game. They surprised everyone and won the conference that year with a 20–6 record overall.

As they compiled win after win, the team renewed excitement and enthusiasm for high school boys' basketball in town, and I was one of their biggest fans. At the age of nine it was fun to be the coach's daughter. But the principal's daughter two years later? Not so much.

Life's not fair

In our small town, the only organized summer team sports for kids were baseball for boys and softball for girls. I wasn't a softball player, so until I was old enough to get a job, summer vacation from school meant long, lazy days doing whatever I liked to keep myself occupied. I slept until nine-thirty and watched TV game shows until lunch time. I read a couple gothic mystery novels a week, and most afternoons rode my bike to the swimming pool with my next-door friend, Lori.

In the evening Lori was my teammate in games against our brothers. We played kickball, kick the can, and Annie-I-over. Those backyard games introduced me to competition, negotiation, and teamwork, but many nights the game devolved into an argument.

"I got you—you're out!"

"No way—you cheater!"

"We're up—get out there and pitch!"

"NO!" Arms crossed.

"You're stupid!" Grass thrown.

"You are!" Balls thrown.

We wanted to continue playing, but no one wanted to concede. Stomping away, I'd find Dad and whine, "It's not fair!"

"Christine," he told me time and again, "life's not fair."

It sure didn't seem fair to my eleven-year-old self. For one thing I didn't have the sister I desperately wanted. But once fall came around and I started attending the junior high, my sense of victimhood grew exponentially. Being the principal's daughter was not nearly as fun as being the coach's daughter. I never thought about what my life would have been like if Dad wasn't a coach and principal. It's just how it was. So I did my best to fly under the radar, which was difficult.

"Chris, there's your dad!" classmates would alert me as we passed his office on our way to gym class. I'd keep my head down and walk as quickly as I could. I didn't need to be reminded of his presence. He started our homeroom with morning announcements over the PA system. He was in the hall between every class change. He supervised everything from sporting events to the end-of-year dance held in our gym.

If I so much as chewed a piece of gum during class, one of

my classmates would act shocked and threaten, "I'm going to tell your dad." I wondered if my teachers talked to him about me, or if they were concerned they'd be perceived by my class-mates as giving me preferential treatment. I was well aware that anything good I did would reflect positively on him, and any-thing bad would be twice as disgraceful. As though junior high isn't awful enough. The combination of my circumstances and my introverted personality earned me the label of "goody-two-shoes," and I was frequently scolded, "Chris, you're *so quiet!*"

Like every other tween-age girl, I had typical friend prob-lems as we sorted out who our real ones were. More than once I was tested by the same group of girls. I wish I'd had the confi-dence to speak up for myself, especially the time they voted on whether or not I should be invited to a slumber party.

One morning in the hall before the first bell, a group of girls stifled their laughter as I approached. Moments before they'd held their heads together, whispering, making plans I would never be privy to. I smiled and walked past them quickly as the familiar knot tightened in my stomach. I suspected they were planning some sort of a party. A party they wouldn't want the principal to know about. Ignorance was a blessing, really. Attending would put me in the awkward position of either lying to Dad to protect my classmates or turning them in. If they invited me and I declined, I would solidify my reputation as a goody-two-shoes. It was a no-win situation.

There were days I couldn't walk home fast enough. I just wanted to hole up in my bedroom, listen to music, and do homework until the comforting smell of dinner drew me out. The six of us always ate supper together and spent the evening gathered in the family room watching television. I felt safe at home. Until the telephone reminded me there were people out there who didn't like Dad.

Sometimes I could tell he was talking with an adult, but one evening, as we watched *Welcome Back, Kotter*, it was clear by the amused look on Dad's face he was getting an earful from a junior high student. He smiled as he put the receiver in the end table drawer until we went to bed. The next day, when he called the kid's mother to apologize for the inconvenience of tying up her line, she assured Dad she'd have a talk with her son and it wouldn't happen again.

Some callers weren't as amusing. During one Sunday dinner, I jumped up from the table to answer the ringing phone.

"Tell Dick he sucks." Click.

"No one was there," I lied to my family as they looked expectantly from the table.

I learned to brush off the phone calls, but I cried when our Halloween pumpkins were stolen off our porch and was sick to my stomach the night tomatoes and eggs were thrown at our house. If someone could do that, I wasn't sure what else they might do to hurt our family. But Dad protected us from most of the unpleasantness.

Almost every season there was a group of disgruntled sports parents trying to get him fired. One morning a player's father appeared at Dad's junior high office. He had come from the local coffee house where everyone at his breakfast table agreed that his son should be getting more playing time. Dad calmly explained that the boy didn't put forth effort in practice and what skills he'd need to work on to earn more playing time.

Thankfully, Dad had the support of the chief administrator who told him, "Well, Richard, you did it again. A school board member called to let me know there's a petition to get you fired. Don't worry about it. As long as I'm superintendent, you'll be the basketball coach."

Years later, Dad laughed about all the heat he took. "I was very fortunate because it was a typical small town—everybody thought they were a basketball player, and I had five hundred assistant coaches."

He knew the criticism was part of the gig. He'd brush it off and focus on teaching the boys the game. He loved the strategy. He loved the reward of teaching a kid a move under the basket and watching him practice until it "clicked" and he could do it in a game. He valued every boy on his team, regardless of skill level, because every role was important, and they were all learning lessons that would pay off in their adult lives. Coaching basketball was about much more than the final score. That it was more than a game was something I understood without being told.

*

Every fall when the season began, our routine shifted. Dad got home from work later, and if the Panthers weren't playing on a Friday or Saturday night, he'd go to another game to scout an upcoming opponent. Because he also attended school board meetings or had other commitments for his role as a principal, there were weeks when my interaction with him was limited to awkward encounters in the junior high hallway. So I welcomed his invitation to join him on scouting trips.

I felt a little like my heroine Nancy Drew as we found an inconspicuous spot in the bleachers to watch the game and look for clues on how to beat the other team. Dad would explain the difference between man-to-man and zone defense or encourage me to observe the beauty of perfect form as a skilled shooter sunk free throw after free throw. I absorbed some of his passion for the game when he talked me through how a team's offense unfolded and what he would do to stop them. And I came to appreciate the significance of an upset—when the team who wasn't expected to win did.

Basketball provided a counterbalance to junior high angst. When I was at a game, I didn't think about friend problems. I didn't worry my behavior was being scrutinized. And I had a way to connect with Dad. I had not yet heard of Title IX. I had no idea that I would soon be dribbling the ball up the court myself. I just loved learning about the game.

Making history with D.D.S.

By the 1974–75 basketball season, Dad's fifth as head coach, he had refined his basketball philosophy such that the foundation for his program was desire, discipline, and structure, or D.D.S. That season defined Dad as a coach and provided numerous lessons that have guided me, an eighth grader at the time, through life.

I was well aware there were high expectations for Dad's team that year. He admitted later that he had felt the pressure because he knew it was possible for the boys to excel. They were great kids, talented athletes, and seven of them were over six feet tall.

His bench was deep, and Dad emphasized the importance of everyone's roles. The competition in the conference was fierce that year; it was crucial that the boys challenged each other every day in practice. The second and third strings were as critical to the team's success as the starters, sometimes more so. During games, those who didn't start had to "have their heads in the game" and be ready to come in off the bench the moment they were needed.

His team could score, but Dad knew that great defense and rebounding would be the key to winning games in the Northwest Conference that year. When asked about the Panthers' prospects, he told the *Freeport Journal-Standard* sportswriter that this was *potentially* the best team Lena-Winslow had ever put on the floor. He knew there were no guarantees when coaching teenage athletes.

The pre-season conference tournament provided the first chance for fans from every community to see just what the competition had that year. Le-Win beat Aquin in the tournament opener by a surprisingly large margin, 63–41. Dad explained their success in a *Freeport-Journal Standard* newspaper article: "We used six different types of defenses (man-to-man and zone variations) and I believe they worked well," said Maher. "We've worked to the point where we can automatically shift to a certain defense, depending on the game situation and where the ball is being played."

We beat Dakota in the second game of the tournament to put us in the championship game against the Galena Pirates. We lost the showdown, setting up the challenge to beat them during regular season play. A few weeks later, heading into the Durand Holiday Tournament, the Panthers had a 6–3 record. We won the first two games in the tourney, earning another championship game slot, only to lose again. This time by one point to Dakota.

By early January it was evident that any team in the conference could win on any given night; most games came down to the final minutes and were decided by fewer than five points.

Dad's Coaching Philosophy
D.D.S.
Desire. Discipline. Structure.

My first experience with learning the importance of **Desire** goes back to my time at Western Illinois University and the classes I took in the athletic department. Just about every class I took, all the coaches would emphasize desire—your athletes must have desire and without it, you weren't going to be very successful.

When I was fortunate enough to get into coaching, I learned that **Discipline** was also important. I'm not talking about behavior discipline, I'm talking about when your players are given positions of responsibility, and they must know their positions and all the aspects of the offense and what they are expected to do, as well as on defense, knowing all of their assignments and the team assignments overall. That in itself is a discipline, to make sure you know, understand, ask questions, and be confident you have the knowledge of all aspects of the game you need to know while participating.

Structure overarches everything. Without structure, you have nothing. Structure includes the method and way you hold your practices, [taking into consideration] the team as a whole and players as individuals and, your philosophy and expectations as a coach. And then the players are held accountable for filling in what they are responsible for.

"I put everything my players needed to know in a handbook: my philosophy, expectations, and every offensive and defensive play—my whole program," Dad said. It was like an individual little bible—most players knew plays and what to do but had never seen it combined in a booklet for their reference. They were to take it home to study it, not at school.

"If your players have D.D.S. and an understanding of a program, you're on the way to the first practice."

- Richard Maher

For me, nothing else mattered on game night. Whatever had happened in my junior high world was forgotten when I left home for the game. I loved the rush of being in the packed gym, the band playing "The Horse" while the boys warmed up, tension rising from the court as boys on each team tried to appear more serious and focused than the rest. Anticipation and adrenaline kept me on the edge of my seat as quarter by quarter we edged our way to victory in the next two games, putting us near the top of the conference standings. We played great basketball until January 10, when we were handed a devastating 51–50 loss to the same Aquin team we had beaten by 22 points to start the season.

I wasn't sure what to say when Dad arrived home that night. I sat at the kitchen table with him, reviewing the scorebook in disbelief.

"Well, Christine, the monkey's off our back."

"What do you mean?"

"The pressure's off. It's harder to stay on top than to get on top. We shouldn't have lost. But sometimes that's the best thing that can happen. Now we can concentrate on playing basketball. We can play to win, rather than not to lose."

I learned later that two of the boys had quit the team that night because they thought they deserved more playing time. Given their negative attitudes, Dad disagreed with them and accepted their uniforms. He'd learned not to talk someone into staying when he wanted to quit.

What could have been a dark night leading to a downward spiral had the opposite effect. Dad put his multiple defenses on the shelf and went back to fundamental basketball, playing primarily man-to-man, which successfully led to an aggressive offense.

Just five nights later we beat the previously undefeated Galena 55–49 on their home court. We went on to win the next seven games, not losing again until the last game of the regular season when Galena beat us at home 83–74. The Panthers ended the regular season third in the conference with an 8–4 record, behind Galena and Lanark, who tied for first with 9–3 records.

"I'm very pleased with our attitude," Dad told the *Freeport Journal-Standard* as his team prepared for the first game of the state tournament. "We decided back on January 11, after a one-point loss to Aquin, that the pressure was off us and that we'd spend the rest of the season trying to improve as much as we could while having fun. That's what high school basketball is all about."

Dad considered the state tournament the second season. Records achieved during the regular season didn't matter. Every team had a clean slate and a chance to progress from their regional games to Assembly Hall at the University of Illinois in Champaign. To "go downstate" was the dream. Teams were assigned to regionals in the two-class system that separated the small from the large high schools. Because regional assignments were determined by geography, we would have to beat some of the same opponents we'd been playing all year.

Our regional was described by the *Freeport Journal-Standard* as "possibly the best balanced, most competitive regional in the entire state," but our Le-Win Panthers sent Orangeville packing 75–55 in the first game, serving notice to the other contenders. Two nights later we beat the top-seeded Shannon Eagles 60–48, marking the second time Dad had won twenty games in one season and earning the team a berth in the championship game against conference rival Dakota.

One of Dad's seniors, Matt Stewart, who had been a starter since his sophomore year, was highly motivated to make it out of the regional after being defeated early on in his first two seasons. In the championship game, a determined Matt did the unthinkable: he made all eleven of his field goal attempts and eight straight free throws to lead the team to a 69–52 victory in Lena-Winslow High School's first ever regional win in the history of the school.

The achievement created a frenzy in every town of our school district. People stopped Dad on the downtown sidewalk to shake his hand. Signs appeared in store fronts wishing the Panthers good luck. I gathered congratulatory cards from our mailbox. Our phone rang with good luck wishes. The Booster

Club chartered two buses to take fans to the sectional game in Port Byron, one hundred miles to the south, the following week. Mom took all four of us on the bus—there was no way we were going to listen on the radio.

The Panthers met the Fulton Steamers in the first game of the sectional. Dad's strategy, based on his scouting report, helped the boys cruise to a 61–52 win.

Two nights later additional buses were chartered for the sectional championship. We were just two wins from "going downstate" to play in the Elite Eight at the University of Illinois in Champaign. More signs went up. Streamers decorated the high school hallways. A pep assembly was planned. Dad urged the boys not to get too caught up in the excitement, to stay focused and continue their usual daily routines.

And on game day Dad followed his. Ray Price on the stereo. A steak. Quiet conversation with Mom at the table. My brothers and I watched as he prepared to leave the house. Dress pants and a short-sleeved shirt. Clip-on tie. Belt slung below his expanding waistline. Wingtip shoes. Sport coat. Wrigley's Doublemint Gum. Scorebook. We wished him luck as he headed for the gym where his team would depart amid cheers from fans whose caravan of cars would follow the team once again to Port Byron. While the boys rode in silence, we on the fan bus chanted cheers and sang the school song.

A sea of black and golden yellow filled the expansive gym, stretching clear to the ceiling. The Riverdale Rams' school colors were the same as ours. And though we were playing on their home court, it looked like we had as many fans as they did. My heart beat along with the thump-thump of drums and blare of horns as our two school bands took turns playing as the boys warmed up.

I was wearing the same pair of jeans and socks I'd worn to each of our wins in the tournament. If we lost, I didn't want to be responsible. A knot tightened in my stomach as I watched our opponents conduct pregame drills. They looked good. Really good. The Riverdale boys came to win. And their coach had done his research. Just minutes into the game, I could tell we were off. We couldn't get our rhythm. Each quarter began with me willing the boys to take control of the game. Each ended with us on the lower end of the scoreboard. We weren't playing our game. We looked desperate. We were playing not to lose.

As the fourth quarter clock wound down, with no chance of a comeback, tears ran down my face. We rode the fan bus home in silence, heartbroken for our team. And ourselves. Riverdale crushed our dreams with a 2–3 zone that shut down Matt Stewart from scoring inside.

I didn't know what to say when Dad got home. I scanned the scorebook that told the painful story in minute detail. Two players made the only four free throws the team had shot. But otherwise the team had made only sixteen baskets, while missing thirty-two.

Dad was calm as he took off his shoes and sat down with me at the kitchen table.

Tears rolled down my face.

"Oh, Christine. It's okay."

"It's not fair. We should be going to Champaign."

"Life's not fair, Christine."

"How are the boys? What did you say in the locker room after the game?"

"I said, 'Fellas, it was a great year. I'm proud of you, and you accomplished a lot. You'll realize that someday. We'll be sad tonight. But tomorrow the sun's going to come up and the cows are going to get milked.'"

A GIRL'S PLACE

Role models

My first female role model, besides my mother and my elementary school teachers, was the mystery heroine Nancy Drew. Nancy was a true-blue friend and dedicated daughter who thought nothing of jumping into her roadster to chase a criminal down a mountainside road. I admired her persistence, logical thinking, and ability to piece together information to solve the crime. Nancy never backed down from a challenge, and she built on her experiences to become a better detective. And she didn't act silly or stupid to get her boyfriend's attention.

My grandmother bought three Nancy Drew books for birthdays and Christmas for both me and my cousin so we could read and exchange them. I devoured all of them but never gave serious thought to a career in crime fighting.

Just as I was outgrowing Nancy, the Mary Tyler Moore show debuted on television. The groundbreaking sitcom's main character, Mary Richards, was pretty and thin, had a stylish professional wardrobe, and lived in a single girl's dream apartment. A wall of windows facing a lake and the Minneapolis skyline, a built-in bookcase tucked into the raised portion of the floor, and a galley kitchen hidden by a pull-down stained-glass window made up for the efficiency apartment inconvenience of sleeping in a hide-a-bed. Mary dated but didn't have a steady boyfriend. She had two best friends and worked in a tall office building downtown. I wanted to be like Mary when I grew up.

While Mary guided my career aspirations, my only opportunity to see women compete in sports was every four years during the Olympics—until Bobby Riggs challenged Billie Jean King to play him in the famous Battle of the Sexes tennis match. At the age of twelve, I had no way to understand the full meaning of that match, or the depth of discrimination and ridicule Billie Jean and her tennis colleagues had endured for years.

As a seventh grader, I watched with Dad as his beloved Boston Celtics beat the Milwaukee Bucks in a seven-game NBA Championship series. The Celtics were loaded with Hall of Famers like John Havlicek, but I chose to cheer for the Bucks, led by Kareem Abdul Jabaar. While other girls hung pictures of David Cassidy and Donny Osmond in their bedrooms, I taped a poster of Kareem, making a hook shot for the Milwaukee Bucks, on the back of my bedroom door.

Playing sports was not even on my radar. I loved school, especially language arts and pre-algebra. I enjoyed singing in chorus, and I gave up my study hall to be a student librarian. By the time I was ready to start high school, I had formed a solid group of friends. Friends who were also good students and with whom I shared a love of reading.

I didn't consider myself to be athletic; the only gym class unit I enjoyed was dance. I was an unlikely prospect to play a "boys" game in front of a crowd. But a year later, there I was, out on the court, prompting some people to question their ideas about what girls would *want* to do as well as what they *could* do.

But my basketball role models continued to be limited to men. When I attended my first basketball camp in the summer of 1976, there wasn't a single female coach, and our guest speaker was an NBA player. Women's Olympic basketball wasn't televised, and I had no idea that coaches like Pat Summitt and Tara VanDerveer were breaking ground as college coaches, learning as they went and doing everything from driving the team bus to washing uniforms to give college women the chance to play.

I enjoyed watching men's college basketball even more than the NBA, especially during March Madness. My favorite college coaches were John Wooden of UCLA and Al McGuire, who led my favorite college team, the Marquette Warriors, to an NCAA Championship in 1977 when they beat Dean Smith's University of North Carolina Tar Heels. Like Dad, McGuire was full of catchy sayings and analogies—pearls of wisdom that coaches shared so many times it was hard to tell who had said them first. After his coaching career, he became an announcer who frequently proclaimed, "It's not over 'till the fat lady sings!"

"What does that mean?" I asked Dad.

"In the opera, there's always a large woman who sings the last song. The show's not over until she has that big finale."

Dad knew as little as I did about opera, but I nodded.

"It means the game's not over until the final buzzer. You never give up, Christine—you keep playing until the end."

My enthusiasm carried over from the back of my bedroom door to the inside of my high school locker door. I taped up news clippings of Kareem, as well as my Marquette heroes, Butch Lee and Jerome Whitehead. I thought it might earn me some credibility with boys in my class, demonstrating I knew something about basketball. Instead, they weren't quite sure what to think about me.

One morning when I arrived at school, a brown paper bag was taped to the outside of my locker. "To Nuts from the guys," was written on the bag in black marker. Inside I found a shiny silver nutcracker. I'm still not completely sure what they intended, but it wasn't a compliment, and it probably came from a place of discomfort with my interest in what was traditionally their game.

They weren't the only ones who weren't sure what to think about girls playing basketball. Even our high school yearbook framed our playing as an intrusion before acknowledging our future:

Girls Become Champs at Basketball

In 1976 women's lib continued to invade Lena-Winslow High School. Over 30 girls slipped into a pair of tennis shoes and began learning the fundamentals of passing, dribbling, shooting, and playing defense in the game of basketball.

Two teams were formed, one at the Junior-Senior level to compete against teams in the Northwestern Conference. The girls have shown a lot of enthusiasm and willingness to learn, therefore, girls basketball should have a bright future at Lena-Winslow High School.

—1976 PANTHERA, THE LENA-WINSLOW
HIGH SCHOOL YEARBOOK

There was a stigma about playing basketball that didn't exist for girls who played volleyball. Some people viewed us as too feminine for basketball, lowering the expectation of how well we'd play a boys' sport. Others saw us as tomboys rejecting "normal" girl behavior. One night, as my boyfriend and I left a school dance, a younger boy we passed by said to his friends, "There goes jock-ette." I ignored the comments. I didn't understand why they even cared. I just wanted to play basketball.

And though there were no women playing basketball on television and no reports of their college games in the newspaper, in the Lena-Winslow High School gym, Paula Miller and the other girls on the varsity team were excellent role models for us younger girls. They loved playing. They worked hard in practice and games. And they had won all six of their games the first year. I couldn't wait for our second season.

Basketball camp

I knew it was a privilege to attend basketball camp the summer before my sophomore year. Mom and Dad were willing to pay my way with the understanding that it would not make me a better player in a week; I would have to come home and practice what I learned. Mr. Kaiser had also given me a skills evaluation, so I knew what to focus on over the summer.

Going to camp came with responsibility—and provided an adventure. I'd never been away from home by myself before. Our family spent weekends at home together. Our vacations were to visit our grandparents. Going to camp was a big deal.

According to the welcome letter I found in my scrapbook, I was one of 200 girls and 575 boys who attended the 11th Annual Campion Championship Basketball Camp run by Don

Gosz in Prairie du Chien, Wisconsin, in 1976. I shared a room with another girl from Lena, and we made friends with our dorm neighbors, but there was little time for socializing. Our time was scheduled from seven a.m., when we were awoken by a shrill whistle, until we showered and fell into bed by ten p.m.

We attended sessions in the morning and afternoon consisting of lectures and drills to reinforce fundamental skills and game knowledge. As the camp handbook promised, we learned about ball-handling and pivoting; terminology and game orientation; rules; free throws, jump balls, and special situations; individual defense/team defense; jumping and rebounding; and how to practice shooting.

The camp booklet also advised: "CAUTION: REPORT ANY INJURY IMMEDIATELY. DON'T TAKE CHANCES. The camp trainer will have office hours at 9:00 a.m., 1:00 p.m., and 6:00 p.m." Back then, the most common injuries were sprained or jammed fingers. An ankle sprain was considered serious. I never even thought about getting hurt.

We were individually videotaped while shooting, and a coach met with us to provide tips to improve our shot. We were assigned to different teams daily, and every night from seven to nine we had the chance to apply what we'd learned in scrimmages.

There were daily contests culminating in championships on the last day: free throw shooting, 21 in pairs, Mikan Drill, and one-on-one by position. Our special guest was NBA player Gail Goodrich. I had seen him play on TV for the Los Angeles Lakers. He had played for John Wooden at UCLA. I listened intently as he talked about the importance of practice, perseverance, and discipline.

I came home from camp and created a home practice schedule, including some of the new drills I'd learned. I counted down the days till school started, then the days till practice would start. Every X on my calendar moved me closer to our second season.

Playing basketball was a physical and mental challenge that I enjoyed. I really didn't care what people said.

Making our mark

While my teammates and I honed our skills as sophomores, joined by the new freshmen, the first varsity girls' team of Lena-Winslow High School roared to another undefeated season. They won all twelve games and earned the conference title. People in our community took notice as we headed into the first State of Illinois Girls' Basketball Tournament. For the last few weeks of the regular season, my friend Beth and I had dressed to play for the varsity games. Mr. Kaiser put us in for the last couple minutes of each game, once a win was assured. We were honored when he posed the question: "Beth Rogers, Chris Maher . . . would you like to dress for the regional?"

We understood it was our responsibility to work hard in practice to prepare the starters. It was highly unlikely we'd get in a game.

The night of our first game, we rode the bus in silence. A much smaller group without the freshman-sophomore team, we wound our way through the hills and turns of northwestern Illinois to the town of Elizabeth, where we would play the host. A handful of parents made the trip to cheer us on. I watched from the bench, wondering if this was the start of a trip like the one Dad's team had taken two years earlier.

By the end of the first quarter we were down 16–11 but rallied to take a 26–25 half-time lead. Paula committed three fouls in the first half, and when she got called for a fourth midway through the third quarter, Mr. Kaiser called me up to go in for her. I was surprised he chose me over a junior, but there was no time to be nervous. He gave me some brief instructions and sent me to check in at the scorer's bench.

I took Paula's place as the point guard and ran the offense. I was relieved to get the ball down the court and into the capable hands of a teammate. Back on defense, I refused to be intimidated. On my second trip down the court, we couldn't get the ball inside to Deb and it came back to me. I shot and was fouled. I missed two free throws but redeemed myself by scoring a basket just before the quarter ended. We had a 44–38 lead going into the last quarter.

Paula returned to the game and the upperclassman held off a surge by the Terrapins. The scoreboard read in our favor, 54–52, when the final buzzer sounded.

Our dedicated fans who filled one small bleacher section cheered, whistled, and clapped. Leaping from the bench, we joined our teammates on the court, jumping up and down, hugging, and high-fiving each other. Paula found me, gave me a hug, and said, "Way to go!" I was relieved I'd played well.

We advanced to play Galena in the next game. It was a well-played game, and Paula stayed out of foul trouble. At half-time we led 17–15. Galena took the lead in the third quarter, and we were down 31–29 going into the fourth. We traded baskets throughout the fourth quarter, but in the end it came down to a made free throw in the final seconds that iced the game for the Galena Pirates, handing the Lena-Winslow varsity girls their first loss in the short history of the program. On the long bus ride home, I resolved to work hard over the summer. Next year, we would beat Galena.

Off track

A couple weeks after the season ended, Mr. Kaiser stopped me in the school hallway.

"Chris Maher, are you going out for track?" he asked, in a way that was clear the correct answer was *Yes*.

I had never run for fun or competition but obediently signed up; track would keep me in shape till the school year ended, when conditioning would become my own responsibility. The track coaches determined the 880 would be a good race for me. Dad agreed, but I wasn't convinced. I had struggled with the 600-yard run in gym class for years. Making it once around the track was doable, but I couldn't set the pace of a 440 runner, so I did what was asked of me.

I tried to find the right balance of effort for each of the two laps. Lap one usually felt okay, but every step of the second lap was a struggle. It was all I could do to put one foot in front of the other and focus on the ground ahead of me until I reached the final curve of the track. At practice and at meets—any time I ran, the knots in my calves tightened as I struggled the last few yards to cross the finish line where a couple teammates waited to walk with me as I cooled down.

Athletic training was in its infancy, and while our "trainer" knew I was low on electrolytes, the salt tablets he gave me were not enough to regain the balance necessary for my muscle fibers to relax. I understand now that I lacked potassium and calcium as well as sodium.

I hated every step of every lap I ran. By the end of the season I promised myself I wouldn't go out the following year and turned my attention to my own off-season conditioning program. Thrilled to be free from the evil track, I planned my morning drills guided by the proficiency and rating chart our assistant basketball coach had given me. I ran wind sprints the length of our driveway, dribbled figure eights around my legs, and practiced reverse layups at our hoop. Every morning. Unless it was raining.

The team members who were available played in an eight-week basketball league at Highland Community College. We organized ourselves, practiced at the park basketball court as our work schedules allowed, and car-pooled for the twelve-mile drive to Freeport one evening each week to play. I'm not sure how much we gained by playing. It was a chance to play as a team in the off-season, but the games lacked excitement and felt more like practice. I looked forward to our real games. Our school games. I crossed the days off my calendar until practice would start.

Varsity!

By the time my classmates and I were juniors playing on the varsity team, the girls had a game schedule similar to the boys'. We played every conference team at home and away; we had several non-conference games; and we played in a holiday tournament.

I was proud to play varsity. Our girls' basketball program had made great strides in just two years. Paula and her classmates had graduated and now it was our turn to represent our school.

The baby brother I'd wished was a sister had become my

little buddy and biggest fan. "Swish 'em, Chris!" five-year-old Michael yelled every time I headed out the door to a game.

On one particular night I especially needed his good wishes. We were playing Galena at home. The crisp cold air cleared my mind, allowing me to focus on our opponents as I walked to the high school under the full moon.

I met up with Beth in the locker room, where we stashed our coats and duffel bags then joined our team in the bleachers to watch the frosh-soph game. But our minds were on our game.

"We. Are. Going. To BEAT these guys," Beth declared, striking her open hand with her fist. We'd lost our first attempt to avenge our regional loss earlier in the season, on their court, 40–33. But tonight was our night. We had a surprise for the Galena girls. Mr. Kaiser had taught us the triangle-and-two defense. While three players set up in a zone to cover the lane, the other two of us would play man-to-man defense on their two excellent guards.

I was going to challenge my player's every pass and every shot. I watched my younger teammates out on the court, but in my mind's eye I was already out there playing defense. As the third quarter ended, we headed to the locker room to change.

In his pregame talk Mr. Kaiser reviewed our assignments with quick reminders of what the players we were guarding would try to do.

"Force her to go left, Beth."

"Deb, don't let her push you under the basket."

"When she gives up her dribble, Amy, help Chris and double-team her."

And finally: "Just like we practiced girls. Just like practice."

The band played Chicago's "25 or 6 to 4" as we ran out of the locker room and made a lap around the gym. During drills, I glanced up to see Dad, Mom, and Michael sitting on the top bleacher. I was grateful they were able to come. Some of my teammates had parents who couldn't get away from the farm or had a second-shift job in a Freeport factory.

When the band played "Sweet Caroline," I knew Mom would be humming. And Michael was ready to count how many baskets I'd make. But I never knew what Dad was thinking. If he ever disagreed with Coach Kaiser's strategy, I never knew. He told me right from the beginning that Mr. Kaiser was my coach, and I was to follow *his* program. Dad said very little after our games. His comments were limited to praising girls who had played well or noticing our improvement. There was no rehash of the game or my performance. He left that to Mr. Kaiser, and for that I am quite grateful.

As the band finished playing our school song, we headed to the bench for the national anthem and starting lineups. I could count on our announcer, Bing Wells, to pronounce my name correctly. At away games they usually said "May-her" with a long *a* instead of a short one. It always annoyed me.

Deb won the jump ball to start the game, and we enacted our game plan quickly. Our surprise defense flustered the Pirates, and we led through the first quarter. During the second quarter, they began to make adjustments. At half-time Mr. Kaiser made his own, but despite our best efforts, they shot well and pulled ahead in the third quarter. As the fourth quarter wound down, we were forced to commit fouls in an effort to get the ball back. But they couldn't miss from the free throw line either, and Galena triumphed again, 47–38. We didn't play them in the regional that year. We had a year to prepare for our last chance to beat them before graduating.

Our team wasn't the powerhouse that graduated with Paula, but we had a winning season with a conference record of 8–6, and we were 12–8 overall. Two of our losses were to the much larger Freeport High School, whose team beat us by twelve in the regional tournament. With the exception of that loss, the most we lost by that season was nine points.

We didn't fill the gym like the boys' team, but we continued to draw curious crowds to our games. Most fans encouraged us, nodding in agreement, "They're pretty good, for girls." Others still found us a source of humorous entertainment. And a few, like the point guard for the boys' basketball team, had the courage to speak up on our behalf.

Girls' Basketball:
No Laughing Matter, by Scott Hawkinson

Girls Basketball at Le-Win has certainly left its mark with the fans, but the fans may be taking the sport the wrong way.

At a recent girls' game every now and then I could hear a few clusters of laughter, not only from the student section but also from the adult section. At half time and at the end of that game, I asked a few people who'd laughed why they did. The most consistent answer I got was, "How many times do you see players in a partial contact sport knock each other down, get up and brush each other off then say, "Pardon me"?

Even though the players mean well, few people take it like that, instead they chuckle at it. Another comment I've heard was, "The girls' games are boring and when something worth laughing about happens, I do. This kind of starts others off. I think the girls hear us laughing and they start to play a little better."

Fans should not compare boys' basketball to girls' basketball since the girls are still building their program. The frosh-soph team gets most of the laughter due to the lack of skill of the game. The girls have no teams in Jr. High and this makes coaching difficult. Frosh-Soph coach Mr. Orr has a rough time but seems to be making headway with the girls.

So the next time you begin to chuckle at the girls, just remember the girls don't have as much experience as do the boys.

—Lena-Winslow High School Panther
Press vol. 12, no. 5, February 17, 1978

We girls on the team appreciated that our classmate took a risk to stick up for us. Years later, Scott told me Mr. Kaiser had made a point of thanking him for his support and letter to the editor of our school newspaper.

The final countdown

I awoke to the Bee Gees serenading me with the theme song from *Saturday Night Fever*. Blue sky and sunshine crept through the slit between my bedroom curtains. I was scheduled to work at five that evening. I had one of the coveted few summer jobs for teenagers as a carhop at the Lena Drive-Inn restaurant. I worked six-hour shifts, five or six days a week. If I worked the day shift, I'd shoot baskets in the driveway after supper. When I worked the evening shift, like today, I'd spend an hour on the driveway in the morning.

I rolled over in bed so I could see the chart on my bulletin board. The growing number of notations in the grid kept me honest about how many wind sprints, shots, and drills I completed each day. Next to the chart was the calendar I used to cross off the days until the first day of practice and the first game of the next season. My last season.

One more song and I'll get up. As Paul McCartney and Wings finished their latest hit, I felt more awake. I got up, got dressed, and headed out to the driveway. The sun was warm, the sky was bright blue, the breeze was light. It was the kind of day that filled me with hope.

I shot a few layups to warm up, then took three steps from the backboard along the right baseline and made a half-circle around the hoop taking short shots. Then I stepped back a foot and repeated the process. My efforts were rewarded with the swish of the net or scolded by a clunk off the rim. It was a meditative routine and a reprieve from the mixed emotions and jumbled thoughts I had about my upcoming senior year.

When school started, I would be doing everything for the last time. I thought a lot about where I might go to college. I was excited about the adventure ahead but knew nothing with my family, friends, and boyfriend would ever be the same. Mom suggested that I go to Highland Community College in Freeport. I knew many of my classmates would go there, but my closest friends were more inclined to go away to college at a four-year school. Plus, I was ready to go somewhere where no one knew I was the principal's daughter.

I was well aware that I would be finished playing basketball unless I joined an intramural team. Paula Miller was playing at Western Illinois University, and her dad thought I could probably be a walk-on, but the idea of playing college ball was overwhelming. I didn't think I was good enough, but I also wasn't sure I wanted to forgo other experiences to devote several hours of my day to the sport. And I wasn't sure how I'd balance the time commitment with homework.

I stood at the free throw line and took fifty shots as the sun rose further in the blue sky; the heat began to rise from the blacktop. By afternoon it would be too hot to shoot. I moved on to ball-handling drills, then finished my workout running wind sprints up and down the driveway.

After a shower and breakfast, I watched TV and read till four-thirty. I grumbled about going to work but was hopeful for a busy night with a couple one-dollar tips, as I'd promised Mom and Dad I'd help pay for my second trip to basketball camp.

My teammate Ruth and I were heading to another of Don Gosz's camps, this time at the University of Wisconsin-Stevens Point. The format for camp was the same as two years prior—drills and lectures during the day, games at night, and contests that culminated on the last day.

I signed up to compete in the free throw and Mikan Drill contests. Each day the contestants competed, the losers were eliminated, and the winners moved on to the next day. I lost to my opponent on the second night of the free throw contest, but thanks to my driveway practice, I beat all of my opponents in the Mikan Drill and found myself one of two girls remaining on Saturday morning.

When it was our turn to face off, I stood below the basket, just as I had so many times in the driveway, ready to step with my left foot and shoot with my right hand. The shrill whistle meant "go," and I found my rhythm quickly. I only missed a shot or two and counted my eighteenth made basket as the buzzer sounded. I turned to the coach who announced I'd won.

I couldn't wait to show Dad my certificate when I found him in the hallway, ready to take me home.

"I won the Mikan Drill!"

Dad nodded. "I know, I saw you. I got here early and was watching from the balcony."

He hadn't made his presence known, and he watched quietly as I competed. But I could tell by his smile that he was proud of me.

Years later I found my Mikan Drill contest winner certificate and the handbook for basketball camp in my high school scrapbook. I'd never forgotten about winning the contest, but I was shocked to see I'd forgotten something much more important. We had heard from a *female* guest player at camp in 1978: Lusia Harris, who had graduated from Delta State in 1975. I was humbled and disappointed in myself when I searched the Internet and read about her accomplishments.

How had I forgotten about her? I had absolutely no recollection of seeing Lusia. But unlike Gail Goodrich, the NBA player who spoke at the previous basketball camp I attended, I'd never heard of her before camp—and I never heard of her after. I couldn't watch her play on television. And there were no posters of her I could hang on my bedroom door. Had there been, she would have served as inspiration as I started my senior year.

Lusia Harris-Stewart

Enshrined 1992 –
Naismith Memorial Basketball Hall of Fame

"One of the greatest centers ever to play women's basketball, Lusia Harris-Stewart was big, relentless, and dominated the painted area like no woman before her. During her four-year career at Delta State University where she played under Hall of Fame coach Margaret Wade, Harris-Stewart changed the face of women's basketball. Opponents called her unstoppable but even that barely described her approach to the game. She scored 2,981 career points (25.9 ppg), grabbed 1,662 rebounds (14.4 rpg), and graduated with 15 Delta State team, single game, and career records. In 1976 alone the bruising center averaged 31.2 points and 15.1 rebounds per game. She led Delta State to a 109-6 record and three straight AIAW national championships. Harris-Stewart was a member of the first-ever women's silver medal Olympic team in 1976, and held the distinction of being the team's leading scorer and leading rebounder."

—Naismith Memorial Basketball Hall of Fame

"The Queen of Basketball," a 22-minute film about Lusia Harris, won the Academy Award for short subject documentary in 2022.

School pride

—————————

Wave the Flag

Wave the flag of Le-Win High School,
Black and gold so grand.
Ever shall our team be victors
Known throughout the land.
U-Rah-Rah
We will always be there fighting,
Without a fear we'll stand.
Wave those grand and dear old colors,
Black and gold for Le-Win High.

—Adapted from "Marching Song,"
by Raymond H. Burke

—————————

Except for football, which hadn't seen success in a decade, all of our sports teams excelled our senior year of high school. Some people started calling it the "Year of the Jock."

That fall our volleyball team infused the most excitement for the Panthers since Dad's regional win. Led by coach Rose Black, they went undefeated in the season and made it to the Elite Eight in the state tournament. As their 22–1 season concluded and our basketball season commenced, our new freshman girls' basketball coach was quoted in a *Panther Press* editorial: "No one can say girls' sports are trivial or unimportant."

Girls' basketball, though, continued to challenge people's thinking. In another article for the *Panther Press*, the same coach stated that coaching the freshman girls "will be very challenging." He had coached boys' basketball for three years in Chicago but said, "The girls are harder to discipline and explain things to. I could joke around with the guys and I don't know how much I can joke with the girls."

The front-page stories of that issue were about the volleyball team's trip to state and an upcoming alumni basketball game the student council would host. Other sports stories included a piece on the success of the wrestling team and a full-page article on the success of the boys' basketball team, which was 8–1 as they headed into the Durand Holiday Tournament, their only loss being to the tournament's host. I'll assume that a print deadline, rather than intentional slight, was the reason there was no story about our Varsity Girls' Basketball Holiday Tournament, because what we accomplished was just as special.

On any given night
On December 18 and 20 we hosted a four-team tournament to prepare us for the conference season that would begin in January. We easily defeated Elizabeth, 41–25, in the first round, while the Rockford East E-Rabs beat East Dubuque. The championship game between us small town girls and the city girls from Rockford enticed more than our usual number of fans to cheer for us that night.

My teammates and I arrived at school early so we could stash our gear in our lockers before the other teams arrived. While East Dubuque and Elizabeth warmed up in the gym for the third-place game, we gathered in the school lobby and assessed our foes as they swaggered down our long school hallway poking fun.

"This is it? This is the whole school? How many people go here?"

"Did you see the cafeteria? Our junior class wouldn't even fit in there."

"Where are we, anyway? It took forever to get here," said one girl as she stopped to fake a dribble and a shot.

Their bravado only fueled our determination. We dressed quietly in the locker room, each of us focused on the game. We didn't play a large school often, but it was a challenge I loved. We could test our skills against a team that presumably had more talent and resources. We had nothing to lose. We were the underdogs, but *any team can win on any given night.*

Mr. Kaiser had prepared us well. Our center, Deb Hardel, was fired up to go head-to-head with East's senior standout, Pat Reck. We were all tuned in and in sync. Thanks to our full-court press, great passing, and Deb's scoring, we jumped out to a 14–7 lead by the end of the first quarter. Both teams scored evenly in the second quarter, and we retained our seven-point lead going into half-time.

We were on a roll and intended to keep rolling, but half-time gave the E-Rabs a chance to reset and change the momentum. They adjusted their defense on Deb and outscored us 14–8 in the third quarter, giving us just a one-point lead with eight minutes left to play.

But Deb wasn't our only threat. When Beth Rogers is determined, there is no stopping her. She led the charge through the last quarter with her rebounding, defense, and a basket that ignited an 11-point run as we stunned the E-Rabs, winning 49–40. Deb had 22 points and Beth scored 13. Three of us combined for another 14 points, but "it was our defense, beautiful defense," Coach Kaiser said of our fourth-quarter rally in a *Freeport Journal-Standard* article titled "E-Rabs Learn Lesson." According to the story, the lesson was "not to mess with coach Marvin Kaiser's girls."

Winning that game—beating Rockford East—boosted our confidence and gave us credibility. We'd had high expectations of ourselves for our senior year and were looking forward to every minute of the conference season. We respected and trusted each other in our roles and were supportive teammates. But, while the outcome of that game would have a long-lasting effect on us personally, our celebrity was short-lived because there was no bigger story than the one the boys' team wrote that winter.

The longest game

Dad resigned from coaching the varsity boys after my freshman year. Between athletic director duties and his own kids' games, something had to go. He wasn't on the bench anymore when the boys played, but now my own classmates were. I continued to be a huge fan. And my knowledge of the game earned me a couple interesting gigs.

To practice for the radio speaking competition at speech contest, I did play-by-play for the boys' games as they were videotaped. It never occurred to me to pursue a career as a sportscaster or sportswriter, but I wonder if I might have had I seen females in those roles. What I enjoyed more—what I loved—was keeping stats. The boys' head coach, Jim Cox, asked a couple of us girls to keep statistics during the boys' games. He appreciated my attention to detail on the shot chart. I plotted the player's number in the precise place the shot was taken, circled the made shots, and quickly calculated the team's shooting percentage at the end of each quarter.

As an added bonus my boyfriend was the center on the team. Sitting behind the team made me feel like I was as much a part of his games as my own. As the girls' schedule expanded, there was some overlap of games, but I continued to keep stats our senior year when we weren't playing on the same night. With the girls' holiday tournament behind us, I was free during the much-anticipated Durand Holiday Tournament.

The boys' conference was very competitive, and we had one of the best teams. Our guys started the season 8–0, but after losing to Durand in a non-conference game the week before, they were determined to beat the hosts in the eight-team tournament. They had their chance when both teams advanced to the championship game.

The team, coaches, and I met at our high school the night of the game. The boys talked quietly as they arrived one by one with their duffel bags and waited patiently for the signal to board the bus. We rode in silence, listening to the engine chug as we traveled the thirty-four miles to Durand in softly falling snow.

We arrived well before game time, and the parking lot was already full. The bleachers filled quickly when the gym doors opened. By tip-off people were standing in the gym corners and shoulder-to-shoulder on the stage, eager to watch the big match-up.

Both teams played tenacious defense, forcing each other to work hard for every basket. At the end of the first quarter, Durand was up 11–10. At halftime we led 20–19. When the final buzzer sounded, we were tied at 32.

As the teams prepared for overtime, I overheard the parents sitting behind me.

"It's snowing to beat the band out there."

"Let's watch the overtime from the doorway so we can get out of here quicker."

But we weren't leaving anytime soon. Both teams scored just two points in the first overtime, and during the next two overtimes, they took turns holding the ball for an unsuccessful last shot. Just before the fourth overtime, state troopers came to the bench and the announcer asked for our attention. "The state police have informed us that road conditions are worsening rapidly. You are encouraged to leave now."

No one left.

The brightly lit gym was electrified with the tension of the game and the threatening weather. The band had long since dispersed, and the cheerleaders implored the crowd to join their chants. Most of the fans were standing, some holding their coats, debating if it was safer to go or stay. Others shook their heads in disbelief, wondering if the game might last all night. The officials wiped their brows; the coaches rolled up their shirtsleeves and loosened their ties, having lost their sport coats an hour earlier. The fourth quarter shot chart had lost its value as I added the overtimes' stats. Finally, I flipped the paper and quickly drew a court on which to record the fourth overtime, thinking it would surely be the last.

At the end of the fifth overtime we were tied at 38, the players were visibly tired, and a couple players had fouled out. Durand, desperate to get the ball, repeatedly fouled Le-Win guard Russ Yeager, who made six of our seven free throws in the sixth and final overtime. We won 45–40.

"Please drive home safely!"

I could barely hear the announcer over our celebrating fans, who poured out of the bleachers to congratulate the boys.

The bus ride home through the snowstorm was not as exuberant as we'd have liked. We rehashed the game in hushed tones so the bus driver could concentrate on getting us home safely. Like everyone in the long line of cars heading back to Lena in the blowing snow, we knew this was a night we'd never forget.

The boys went on to complete an amazing season with a 27–3 record. They also won the conference and a Thanksgiving tournament. They won the state regional and sectional, and came within one game of going to state, losing in the super-sectional game by just one point. But their success had more to do with their bond than with talent, and their coach, Jim Cox, knew that. My classmates' team was like Dad's 1975 team—nice kids, good students, with varying degrees of athleticism. In an interview, Coach Cox explained:

"We don't have a lot of natural ability. We've been fortunate this year but we also have worked hard. These kids have worked so hard that it's hard to describe the pleasure of coaching them. . . . Unity is the thing that makes a basketball team. It's the name of the game. This is a close group of boys and they play that way."

—1978 NEWSPAPER CLIPPING,
PAPER UNKNOWN

While the boys continued to win, we girls also won our next five games in January. There was a friendly camaraderie, respect, and support between the boys' and girls' teams. Sometimes

Mr. Kaiser would ask the boys to practice with us to prepare for a tough opponent. They didn't take it easy on us, and we didn't back down from their challenges.

H-O-R-S-E

I took a fifteen-foot shot on the left wing and hit nothing but net.

"I've got time for a game of HORSE," the starting point guard said, as he threw his duffel bag on the stage. He was the first to arrive for the game bus. The boys were playing at Aquin that night. I was one of the first girls warming up before practice, shooting at the basket in front of the stage.

"Sure," I said, tossing him the ball.

"You first." He tossed it back.

Because I'm a girl? I wondered briefly, but he was not condescending. This was the same guy who'd written the letter to the editor about showing the girls' team more respect. He'd been to our games and helped with our practices. He knew I could challenge him.

I sank one of my patented fifteen-footers, which he matched.

I took another shot a couple feet behind the top right corner of the free throw line. He missed. "H," he said.

I missed my next attempt, but matched his jump shot on the right wing. A few more boys arrived and hopped up to sit on the stage and watch us. "C'mon, Hawk," one offered, though clearly there was no doubt he'd win. He took great pride in playing great defense, but he was also an excellent shooter. He made, and I missed, the next two shots before he missed an attempt. "H to H-O," he said, tossing the ball to me.

My boyfriend arrived to wait for the bus. "Go, Chris! Go,

Hawk!" he encouraged us. He was my biggest fan, but Hawk was his teammate.

I made a shot along the left baseline and watched as Hawk's rolled around the rim before tipping out. I moved out to the left wing, halfway to the free throw line, and smiled a little as the ball swished softly through the net. I was getting into my rhythm.

By this time most of the varsity and frosh-soph boys' teams had arrived. They stretched across the length of the end line, seated on the stage or standing in the corner. I focused on the game, trying to ignore the twenty spectators. My teammates shot at other baskets to warm up for practice. I'm not sure if any of them were watching closely, but I knew some of the boys were. I kept my head in the game, concentrating on one shot at a time.

We traded baskets from the baseline to the top of the circle until the game was tied at H-O-R-S. Hawk also remained calm. There was no taunting, no words exchanged, just focus and respect for each other's opponent, like a game of chess.

He missed his next attempt at a twenty-footer from the right side, forty-five degrees from the basket.

My turn. I returned to my sweet spot on the left wing. I dribbled twice, then just as Dad had taught me, raised the ball with my fingers on the seam. Aiming four inches above the rim, elbow in, bending my knees, I followed through as I came up and released the ball. Swish.

He took my place on the court and shot. The ball rolled around the rim. And fell off.

"You win. Good game." Hawk grabbed his duffel bag from the stage and joined his teammates as they headed to the bus.

"Thanks!" I said, as calmly as I could. *Oh my God, I just beat Hawk.* "Good luck tonight!" Probably not the best way to see our starting point-guard off to a big game. But, I've never believed in letting someone win.

And I must not have bruised his ego too badly. Eight years later, he married me.

A life lesson

Though most of my memories of playing basketball are good ones, I know there were plenty of times I made dumb mistakes or had an off night and left the gym disappointed in myself. And forty years later I clearly remember the time Coach Kaiser *really* yelled at me.

We were playing our archrival Aquin Catholic High School in Freeport, but for some reason had to play our game in a small elementary school gym. The court was smaller than regulation size. The distance from the free throw lane to the sideline was half the norm, and the top of the circle was just a few feet from the mid-court line. The lighting was dim and the place reminded me of our elementary school gym where the boys used to play at lunchtime. Nothing felt right, and I had trouble getting into the game.

So did my teammates. We should have been able to gain a lead from the start, but we were playing poorly and losing. Mr. Kaiser's patient demeanor disappeared by half-time when he sternly reminded us of what we already knew. But as the third quarter began things didn't go much better and he called time-out.

He was angry. And loud. He directed us to take our time and work the ball inside. I walked back onto the court feeling anxious. I didn't want to let him down. Aquin scored, and the next time down the floor our point-guard, Susi, passed me the ball in my sweet spot on the right wing, and I took a twenty-foot shot that clunked off the rim. I knew it was a mistake the moment the ball left my hands. In the moment I just wanted to score for my team, and I panicked.

The ref's whistle blew as Mr. Kaiser called time-out.

"Chris Maher, what are you doing?" he roared. "Didn't I just tell you not to shoot outside?"

He moved on to address my teammates, repeating the instructions he'd given us in the time-out just two minutes earlier, then sent us back on the court to try again.

Later, I talked about the incident with my friend and teammate Beth. She said when Mr. Kaiser yelled at us in that time-out, she went back out on the court fired up and determined. I went back out on the court afraid to make another mistake. I wasn't able to gain any traction on the court that night and deservedly spent most of the rest of the game on the bench.

Like coaches, every player has a unique personality and a perspective shaped by their upbringings and their own life experiences. On the court, as in life, we all face challenges that force us out of our comfort zone or remind us that the world doesn't revolve around us. Things are not always going to go our way.

I went to the next practice determined to do better.

Benched

For over three years I had looked forward to each season. To each practice. To each game. Day after day I did what was asked of me and challenged myself in the off-season to improve. I didn't want to let my teammates or Coach Kaiser down. We had all improved significantly since our first year. By our fourth season my teammates and I had grown beyond routine execution of plays, and we had developed an understanding of the game.

By mid-February our record was 11–2, and I began to feel a sense of urgency as I saw my final season disappearing on the calendar. Our only losses had been to conference rivals Dakota and Galena, but we had another shot at both of them. When February arrived, I was completely focused. My playing days were coming to an end. I never imagined they'd end before the season did.

For some reason—maybe one of them was rescheduled due to a snowstorm—we had three games the week of February 13. On Sunday I looked forward to the fun week ahead: three games for us, plus a conference showdown for the boys, whose regular season ended that Friday night. My team beat Orangeville easily 52–39 on Monday night, but I felt winded. It wasn't acceptable to run out of steam late in the game this late in the season. So on Tuesday I stayed after practice to run the halls an extra half hour. I felt better Wednesday, and we beat Aquin 51–36. But my stomach ached a bit when I got home that night. Thinking I was hungry, I ate some oatmeal before going to bed.

On Thursday, we won our third game of the week against Pearl City, 65–50. By the time I got home my stomach ached again but I had no interest in food. I went to bed with a hot water bottle for comfort, but jabbing pain woke me a couple hours later. I called Mom and she entered my room just as I tried to stand but instead doubled over. She woke Dad and helped me get dressed. A few minutes later Dad and I were on our way to the Freeport Memorial Hospital emergency room.

I held my hand tightly against my stomach but couldn't take the edge off the pain.

I'd never been to the hospital as a patient. The exam room was dim and cold. The nurse talked quietly and reassured me as she wrapped a warm blanket around my shoulders and drew some blood from my arm. Dad and I said little as we waited and watched the minute hand slowly circle the clock. It was almost three a.m. before we learned I had a high white blood cell count; I had an infection due to appendicitis. Dad went to fill out papers while the nurse took me to a room via wheelchair. I changed into a hospital gown and got into bed to be prepped for surgery. I was afraid but watched curiously as one nurse started my IV and another told me what would happen next. A surgeon was on his way, and they would take me to the operating room soon. They would place a mask over my face to put me out. I wouldn't feel anything, and I'd wake up in the room I was in right now. They were going to remove my hot appendix as soon as possible.

When I came out of surgery Dad went home and brought Mom back with him. They were in my room when I awoke nauseous from the anesthesia. I held tight to the bandage on my stomach when I vomited and was grateful for the pain medication that put me back to sleep. Mom and Dad sat with me until they had to go home to my brothers. The nurse assured them I would sleep most of the next twenty-four hours, but I insisted I needed a radio to listen to the boys' game and asked her to be sure I was awake at game time.

I drifted off a couple of times during the game but managed to stay awake for the last quarter as the boys won the conference championship. As the announcer described the celebration in the gym, he said, "We hear one of the Panthers' biggest fans, Chris Maher, is in the hospital tonight. We know you're excited but don't celebrate too much—no running up and down the halls—and get well soon!"

I wish I could have gotten well soon.

In 1979 appendicitis meant a five-inch incision, several stiches, and weeks of recovery. I spent five days in the hospital, diligently working on my term paper for Mrs. Miller's college preparatory English class as the truth sank in. I was done playing basketball.

Christine, life isn't fair.

When I returned to school, nothing felt right. I attended classes, did my homework, and used my books as a shield from getting run into by accident in the hallways. I watched my teammates practice, feeling sad and disconnected. My primary anchor at school was gone, and I could see everything else would also slip away in the three months until graduation. By the time June arrived, there would be no more speech contest. No more hanging out in the hallways with my friends. No more school dances. Life as I knew it was coming to an end.

I became moody and angry, snapping at my boyfriend and my friends. I tried to support my teammates and continued to keep stats for the boys, but I couldn't find anything to be happy about.

The boys' state tournament schedule was a week ahead of the girls' and odds were they would win the regional. I didn't want to think about the potential overlap of games and reacted badly when faced with the question.

"Chris Maher, what are you going to do if the boys'

sectional game is the same night the girls play in the regional?"
Mr. Kaiser asked.

"I'll probably go to the boys' game."

"What do you think your teammates will think if you do
that? You're still part of this team."

"I don't feel like I am."

"If you don't feel like you're still part of this team, then I
haven't done my job."

Of course, Mr. Kaiser had done his job. My season-end-
ing surgery had added another emotional layer to the fact that
seventeen-year-olds can be shortsighted and selfish. I certainly
was that day.

The next day after school as I did homework Dad came into
my bedroom and shut the door. I knew it was serious—he'd
never done something like that.

"Listen, I'm hearing all kinds of rumors about what happened between you and Mr. Kaiser. What happened? Did he
kick you off the team?"

"No! I told him I'd quit if I had to choose between the boys'
and girls' game." I was embarrassed and horrified Mr. Kaiser
was taking the blame for my behavior.

Dad listened and nodded as I told him about our conversation. He let me come to my own conclusion about what to
do next, but I certainly knew what he'd want his player to do.

I apologized to Mr. Kaiser and continued to support my
teammates, who won four more games and lost two to finish
the regular season. Our final buzzer sounded when we lost to
Galena for the third time that year in the regional championship. Our final record was 15–5.

As it turned out, there was no conflict with the boys' games, and I was able to support both teams through the end of their seasons. If I had been forced to choose between games, I would be ashamed to this day if I hadn't supported my teammates.

I was voted a co-captain of the team my senior year and had received a sportsmanship award as a junior. But the most meaningful recognition was when Mr. Kaiser gave us plaques that deemed Amy Kopko, Beth Rogers, Ruth Schwartz, and me—the first four girls to play four years of girls' basketball—"Pioneers of Lena-Winslow High School Girls' Basketball."

*

The girls on my team came from various family backgrounds and friendship groups. Some of our paths would never have crossed had the landmark law Title IX not brought us together. We never beat Galena, but we succeeded in ways that can't be recorded in a scorebook.

We learned what it meant to be part of a team. About commitment and loyalty. We learned the importance of building a strong foundation with fundamentals. About practice and perseverance. We learned that there is no easy road to accomplishment. And that adversity makes you stronger and more determined.

I was more ready to go to college than I realized. And though I was also prepared to close the basketball chapter of my life, that book was far from finished.

ROLES

THE COACH'S WIFE

Jump ball

On August 25, 1979, Mom, Dad, Michael and I backed out of the driveway in the small blue pickup truck Dad had borrowed from a friend. I'd carefully packed my most prized possessions: over fifty record albums and my four-in-one stereo that housed not only a radio and turntable but a cassette *and* eight-track tape player. Other than that I only needed a few dorm room decorations, the electric typewriter I'd received for a graduation gift, and my clothes. As we headed down the street, I watched the basketball hoop, my brothers' treehouse, and the home I grew up in disappear from sight. I knew that nothing would ever be the same again.

I'd mastered high school and helped launch girls' basketball, but college was going to be an entirely new game. Once again I'd have to learn the fundamentals and understand my role before I could begin to thrive. Thanks to the women's liberation movement, I considered careers that my mother and grandmothers never imagined. Word was that women were entering the business field in droves and that businesses were doing more to hire them. Over and over, teachers and friends of my parents told me I'd certainly get a good job and I'd earn good money as an accountant—as a *woman* in accounting—as though my gender would ensure respect and success.

I learned to take good notes and how to study for college exams. I got good grades but was lost and lonely my sophomore year after I broke up with my boyfriend, my best friend announced she was not returning to school in January, and my roommate friendship was strained as she dealt with some personal problems. When a panic attack sent me to the campus counseling office, I received advice as memorable as the advice from my econ professor: "You need to have five connections to feel like you belong here. That includes friends and classes, but joining an organization or club will give you a greater sense of belonging. Check the bulletin boards and read the student newspaper carefully. When you see something of interest, try it out, get involved."

Four weeks later I became the assistant treasurer for University Union Board, or UUB, the student-run programming board that booked events ranging from speakers and coffeehouse acts to movies and rock concerts. The personalities of the dozen board members were as diverse as our programming, and anyone who was interested could join the committees. When spring elections came up, I ran for the treasurer position on the executive board, won, and assumed that role for my junior year.

Outside of class, my days revolved around the work, friendships, and camaraderie of UUB. I looked forward to our weekly board meetings the way I'd looked forward to game nights.

I was part of my first real coed team, learning about leadership and roles. Unfortunately, things didn't go as well in my advanced accounting classes. I didn't enjoy what I was learning, and my heart told me I was on the wrong path.

The idea of earning a communications degree crossed my mind. But I failed to explore this possibility with someone in the department, and I didn't realize there were many ways to earn a living as an editor or writer. I was also determined to graduate in four years and knew the change would add a year or more to my studies. I stayed in the business school, changed my major to marketing, and went to summer school so I could graduate on time.

Two weeks before graduation I accepted a job with Osco Drug Company, and two weeks later, I moved to Indianapolis to begin working as a management trainee in one of their stores. I felt like Mary Richards, but my apartment wasn't near as cool. And I never felt quite as welcome at Osco as Mary did at the television station.

I had assumed the work world would be similar to Union Board—diverse, collaborative, accepting. The reality was that I was going to have to prove myself just like I'd done on the basketball court.

"You're so young!" the cosmetics department manager, a mother and grandmother in her fifties, said as she looked me over, shaking her head. She was the first person I met when I reported to my first professional job. "Well, I wish you good luck."

"They say they want women in management, but it takes women a really long time to get a store, if they ever do," shared a young man who was working his way through college with part-time employment at our store.

At first I was determined to be one of the women who made it. But as the months passed, I didn't enjoy the work or the lifestyle it required. With every promotion, assistants at all levels, as well as store managers, were moved to a different store, usually in a different city. In fourteen months I worked for five managers in two cities.

I left the company and spent the next nine months spinning my wheels. After an unsuccessful job hunt in Indianapolis, I realized I wanted to live closer to my family. When I called Mom to tell her I was moving home, she had some interesting news for me as well.

"Scott Hawkinson called here looking for you the other day. He's working at the school and was asked to chaperone the prom. He wondered if you'd like to go with him."

And that's how, six years after beating Hawk at that game of H-O-R-S-E, we began dating. It was prophetic that our classmates had voted us king and queen of our own prom. Within a few weeks I knew that we were meant to be together.

*

"I hope your marriage lasts four quarters and six overtimes," Scott's high school coach, Jim Cox, said, congratulating us in the receiving line at our wedding.

Everything else seemed to suddenly fall into place. I got a job in Rockford, and Scott was hired to teach elementary PE and coach varsity boys basketball for the Bulldogs in nearby Durand. We were able to rent a home not far from the school and just a twenty-minute drive from my job.

While I continued to struggle to find my team in the work world, I fully embraced the role of coach's wife. My experiences as a player and coach's daughter provided a solid foundation for understanding what was happening with Scott's team beyond what people saw on the court.

We brought our knowledge of the game and youthful enthusiasm to Scott's new role, but basketball was an afterthought in the small town that had recently been the runner-up in the state football championship. The principal told Scott he should try to keep the games interesting so students wouldn't cause problems in the hall and cafeteria during play.

A week before their first game, and Scott's debut as varsity coach, he scheduled an open house and scrimmage to introduce himself to the boys' parents and show them what the team had been working on in practice. I sat alone on the top bleacher, taking in the scene below.

Parents wondering who this young guy was coaching their sons.

Boys deciding if they would buy into his ideas.

A young coach influenced by his own coaches and others he admired.

Scott is a strategist; he loves to analyze the game, decipher the opponent's offense and defense, and create plays to shut them down. I often went along when he scouted opponents, keeping stats so he could make other observations. I attended every game and kept the shot chart just as I had for our high school team. It helped me focus on the game and watch for things to discuss with him later.

Scott is also very competitive. Like Dad, he prepared to win, and his motivation came from wanting his players to succeed, both individually and as a team. He knew a successful team needed talent, but more importantly they needed to be committed to working hard for themselves and their team. They had a responsibility to put the team first. But kids don't always do that.

You choose the behavior, you choose the consequences

Scott's teaching schedule was jam-packed with ten elementary PE classes in a row. With lunchtime duties, he barely had time to eat his own. So when our receptionist told me he was on the phone for me in the middle of a January day, I knew something was wrong.

"Hey there. I thought I'd better let you know what's going on. I found out today that four of my players were partying over the weekend. There were witnesses, and I had to tell them they are off the team."

"Oh, no . . . Who?"

Scott named three of the boys and paused before stating the name of our landlady's son.

My stomach did a flip.

"Okay, good luck. Let me know if I should start looking for a new place to live," I said, only half-joking.

The players code of conduct was straightforward, guided by these truths: playing a sport for your school was a privilege, not a right; there were rules; if you broke the rules, there were consequences. Scott enforced it quickly.

The parents of the four boys acknowledged their kids had broken the rules and expected the discipline that followed. There was no outcry that they should be given a second chance or that the incident would ruin their lives. Parents of the boys remaining on the team were supportive and understanding. Lessons were learned, and life went on.

My game plan

Despite the challenges, Scott loved coaching and enjoyed teaching—particularly teaching the elementary school kids, who were always saying something cute and appreciated his corny sense of humor.

But while he was comfortable with his work role, I was not comfortable in mine. In just seven years in the workforce I had encountered stereotypical good old boys, women who hadn't learned we need to support each other, and a boss who thrived on creating conflict. The women who might have mentored me were not respected by the men in charge. I wanted to be a pioneer for women at work as I had been on the basketball court, but I didn't even like the actual work. I had no desire to fight for the right to be there.

The only team I could believe in was the one I was building with Scott. While expecting our first baby, we decided it was time to move on from Durand. Scott was ready for a new challenge, and I was ready for a new adventure. I typed nearly forty cover letters for Scott while I was home on maternity leave. He got one interview, an offer the next day, and started work two weeks later in Dodgeville, Wisconsin.

I never set out to marry a man like my father, and I had sworn I would never let my kids go to school where their dad worked. Yet we were about to replicate my parents' life in oh-so-many ways. Like Dad, Scott was a teacher and coach. And I had decided to focus on a role I'd had an excellent role model for: mother, homemaker, and coach's wife.

*

Coaches rely on their assistants to scout opponents, work with individual players to improve their skills, and help run drills in practice. And coaches rely on their spouses to keep their households running, take over most parenting duties, and provide mental support during the season. As a teenager I was oblivious to the load Mom carried while we were growing up.

"Mom?!" we'd all call when we walked in the door from school. After a quick check-in, we'd watch TV, do our homework, or run outside to play. Mom was always home, an anchor for the rest of us when we went out into the world.

Mom ran our household like Dad ran his team—with a defined plan. She cleaned the house on Tuesday and Thursday. She washed laundry on Monday, Wednesday, and Friday. She planned menus, shopped for groceries, and prepared the dinner we ate together, most nights at five-thirty. I'd seen Mom on bill-paying day and understood even as a kid that there were months when Dad's salary was stretched thin to support the six of us, but she juggled as necessary to manage the household budget.

In addition to being homemaker and primary parent, Mom supported Dad by learning the rules of basketball and listening to his endless stories about games, players, and strategies. Visits to her family and our holiday plans revolved around the team's schedule. My brothers and I joked as adults that she should have been listed on the game programs as one of Dad's assistant coaches, but that title was insufficient, as I would learn for myself.

Common wisdom said I was committing career suicide by stepping off the ladder. But once Scott and I agreed how we wanted to raise our children, I was all in, ready to trade money for time. Seven years in the workforce had taught me to be productive and efficient, and I applied my organizational and business skills to running our home.

Like Mom, I completed the household chores on a schedule during the day so we could enjoy family time in the evening and on the weekends. And I budgeted expenses to the penny, as my biggest challenge was to make sure we lived within our means.

Our lifestyle choices taught us to find joy in small pleasures. When our two-and-a-half-year-old daughter was joined by a sister, I pulled them in the wagon up and down our hilly streets. On Wednesdays we went to the library for story time and a dozen new books, followed by a stop at the Corner Drug Store where we could each get a pretzel rod and a mini cherry coke from the soda fountain and receive change back from a dollar. We made a final stop at the Wilson Park playground before heading home for lunch and naptime. This was our favorite day of the week.

Before we'd had children, it was easy for me to attend all of Scott's games, both home and away. If he had an away game, I'd change from my business suit into jeans after work, grab a sandwich at a drive-thru, and drive the thirty- to forty-mile distance. But like Mom, I did not attempt to take the girls to away games. If ours was on the radio, I listened as intently as I had to Dad's away games.

And like Mom, I learned to adjust to the in-season routine in our home. Scott was out the door before seven-thirty in the morning and home around six-thirty in the evening on the days when practice followed the school day, and anytime between nine and eleven at night twice a week on game nights or when he went scouting.

The evening following game day, after the girls went to bed, we watched game films and recorded stats, with me doing the shot chart as I had in high school. Some nights Scott researched new plays or offenses that his team might be well-suited for. He'd run ideas by me, or we'd talk about team dynamics and player or parent issues as they came up. Other nights he was so exhausted he dozed off in his chair and we were in bed at eight-thirty.

Sometimes there were house or personal issues I wanted to discuss but put off, night after night, week after week, as there never seemed to be a good time to talk. I ran our household and handled everything I could so Scott could relax or play with the girls when he did have free time.

There were times I felt like a single parent, but the high school basketball schedule also gets long for coaches and their players, especially if the team isn't doing well. It feels even longer to young children who don't see much of their father. The night our four-year-old had a meltdown demanding that "Daddy should come home right now!" I resolved to plan a mid-season "Kidnap Daddy Weekend" every year to ensure that for at least a couple of days during the season, we'd have some family fun.

I knew I'd return to work full-time at some point, but for now I was living the life of Mary Maher, not Mary Richards. And that was fine with me.

THE COACH

Dodgeville High School Song

Hail to thee, o' Dodgeville,
All orange and black.
Forward our motto, never turning back!
U-rah-rah!
Lead us on to victory, our goal's the sky
Fighting forever for Dodgeville High!

—LYRICIST UNKNOWN

Go, big D!
I could feel the buzz of energy coming in waves from the high school, just a couple blocks from our house. People had been standing in line, bundled in down coats and extra blankets, since the wee hours of a frigid Wisconsin morning to buy tickets to the boys' basketball sectional game. Downtown, people had

gathered to decorate storefront windows while I decorated our home. Three-year-old Lauren helped me gather poster board, markers, and black and orange crepe paper as four-month-old Kylee watched from the baby swing.

"Why are we making things, Mommy?" Lauren asked.

"The Dodger boys are playing in a really important game this weekend. If they win, they will play again, and if they win *that* game, they will play in Madison at the Field House where the Badgers play!"

She didn't understand the details, but she understood there was a reason to be excited. She colored some basketballs on a sheet of white paper to create a good luck card for Scott while I worked on posters for our living room windows. I sang the school song over and over to expend my own nervous excitement. Before long Lauren joined in with her own interpretation of the lyrics:

Hail to thee o' Dodgeville
All orange and black
Lead us on to Vick Street
All gold's the sky!

All gold's the sky, indeed! It had been nearly thirty years since our small town was this excited about basketball. In 1964, before there were divisions for school sizes, an undefeated Dodgeville team led by Coach John "Weenie" Wilson beat the big city school of Milwaukee North 40–39 for the state title. Many of the parents and fans of this 1992–93 team had been in high school at the time; some played on the team. Anyone who knew the story was eager to share their memories as they relived the excitement through this new group of boys. There will never be a greater Dodgeville basketball story than the one of '64, but this one was going to come close.

Varsity coach Chuck Tank had been hired by the district at the same time as Scott; Scott became his assistant/JV coach. Together they had transformed the boys' basketball program in just three years. The first two were pretty rough. It had been fifteen years since the boys had won a conference title, and the year before we arrived, the kids had lost one beloved teacher/coach to cancer and another to a heart attack during half-time of a game. The community was aching for something to be excited about. It was the perfect time for something new and different. Like Chuck's basketball program.

Unlike the methodical game the Dodgers had played in the past, Chuck introduced a fast-paced game that relied on a free-flowing offense rather than set plays. There were a lot of skeptics, especially when the first season ended with an 8–13 record. It would take a special group of kids to demonstrate the possibilities of Chuck's program; even Scott wasn't entirely sold. Like Dad's, Scott's coaching system was more structured. But in the second season, the boys produced a 13–8 record, giving Dodgeville its first winning season in ten years. And this year—magic: the right combination of coaching, talent, attitude, and desire.

I had to look no further than our seats at home games to see the impact of this team on the community. There were no reserved seats like we'd had when Dad coached, so when we got to the gym on the night of our first game in Dodgeville, Chuck had advised his wife Becky and me to sit behind the team rather than in the parents' section, to spare our feelings from the inevitable coaching criticisms.

The seats Becky and I chose that night became ours for the next several years: up about five rows, midway between the team and the stage so our kids had a great view of the band and we could keep one eye on them as the other looked down the court at the action. We had plenty of room to spread out toys and coloring books for Becky's older children—Wes, who was six, and Alli, two. We held our babies, Ann and Lauren, on our laps.

But just two years later, as the boys won game after game, the crowd had grown and soon we sat shoulder-to-shoulder in the tightly packed bleachers with just enough room to seat our preschoolers at our feet so they could use their bleacher seat in front of them to hold their coloring supplies and snacks.

This group of boys believed in Chuck's system; they had worked hard in practices and games. And it was paying off. Game after game, win after win, more fans became believers. But the night the boys ended Cuba City's thirty-two-game conference winning streak, winning 89–59, the home crowd was just as stunned as the Cuba City team was. This Dodgeville team was incredible. There were no more questions about the style of play. People drove from other towns to watch our team play, and our fans beamed with pride. We finished the regular season with a 23–1 record.

A week later we won the first boys' basketball regional since 1978, and the community rallied like it was 1964. Good luck signs appeared in stores downtown and the windows of many homes. Congratulatory and good luck cards arrived in our mailbox. People stopped Scott in the post office or at the grocery store to shake his hand and offer good wishes and thanks for the joy the team had brought to the community.

Scott and I were on our own adrenaline rush, experiencing as adults what we'd enjoyed as students. We talked about Dad's 1975 regional win and our high school team's journey to the Sweet Sixteen in 1979. We knew the experience would be one the boys would never forget and shared in the joy and excitement of the fans. And there wasn't a group more deserving. They were not only a great team, they were great kids. Good students. Respectful. We joked they'd be the kind of boys we'd want our daughters to date someday.

A friend volunteered to stay with the girls so I could go to the sectional games. We beat Evansville in the first game, 76–65, to move on to the championship and the chance to go to state. The frenzy in town grew; there were fewer tickets available than people who wanted to see the game. The general admission seats sold out in under an hour, and the focus shifted to game day.

"What time does the game start?"

"When do the doors open?"

"When should we get there?"

"An hour before game time?"

"But people are saying two hours—"

"No, I heard three!"

As Becky and I discussed our plans with our neighbor, her husband only half-jokingly told us we needed to get a life. We exchanged glances, shrugged, and said, "This *is* our life!"

There would be room in the gym for all who had a ticket, so the nervous anticipation in the days before the game wasn't really about not getting in. Something else had people decked out in black and orange from head-to-toe. Something else had them grinning from ear to ear and resurrecting cheers from their own high school days. Something else made reasonable people stand in the freezing cold for two hours before school officials would open the doors to the gym.

The team had transformed the town. There was a sense of camaraderie and community pride that drew hundreds of us to gather in anticipation of the game. We stood in a long line on the narrow sidewalk leading to the entry doors, walking in place in the frigid cold and telling stories to pass the time. And the boys made it all worth it. We beat Blair-Taylor 88–72 that day. We were headed to state. They'd accomplished what Dad's team and Scott's team had fallen just short of, and Scott and I got to claim a little bit of their success for ourselves.

Ticket-mania grew, but there would be room for anyone and everyone who wanted to go to the game at the University of Wisconsin Field House the following week. It seemed like everyone in town planned to go. Carpools were organized. Fan buses took kids from the schools. The forty-five-mile distance to Madison made it easy for our fans to outnumber those of most of the other schools. Sitting in my seat at the Field House, my heart swelled as I scanned the sea of orange and realized how this team had inspired and energized us all.

Just two hours later our hopes and dreams evaporated as we lost to Auburndale, who went on to win the 1993 Division 3 Championship. But we didn't love those boys any less. In fact, we loved them even more as we watched them play with determination and heart until the final buzzer.

Sports are about so much more than winning trophies.

Coach Hawk

When I started dating my husband, I had a hard time calling him Scott. He'd been "Hawk" to me the eight years we'd gone to school together. In our small class of ninety students, we knew each other, but we had hung out with different crowds, prompting one high school classmate in our wedding receiving line to exclaim, "Who woulda thought you two would get married!" On the surface we seemed as mismatched as my parents. But like Mom and Dad, it was our core values and life choices that provided a sound foundation for a relationship. That, and basketball.

Sometimes I wondered who was happier that Scott came into my life, me or Dad. When we began dating and I was at my parent's home on a weekend, Dad would ask if Hawk was coming for Sunday dinner. I could barely greet Scott at the door when Dad would call from the family room, "Hawk, get down here—the game is on!"

Thus began a thirty-three-year friendship between my father and my husband, cemented while watching hundreds of games on TV. They discussed the strategies and personalities of hundreds of coaches, including the ones Dad called "egotistical assholes," but mostly the legends who helped shape his own philosophy, like John Wooden of UCLA, Al McGuire of Marquette, and Rollie Massimino of Villanova. Scott and Dad were both big Duke and Mike Krzyzewski fans, and Scott always admired Bob Knight of Indiana (despite his outrageous behavior later in his career) for his knowledge of the game and emphasis on defense.

Through the 1990s they observed the gradual shift in the way the game was played. In an effort to "be like Mike," many players began to put fancy before fundamentals, ignoring the fact that NBA star Michael Jordan had built a strong foundation first. Ironically, the increasingly faster pace of the game required greater mastery of dribbling, passing, and shooting the ball. Dad didn't hesitate to call out the lack of fundamental skills, as though the players could hear him.

"Block out! You've got to rebound!"

"Move your feet on defense. You're getting beat every time."

"Shoot the ball! Oh, come on—that's not how you shoot a basketball!"

"Scott, did I ever tell you about Max Zaslofsky? Now, *there* was a shooter!"

There was also a shift in attitude among many players. Some seemed to think the game was about them. The growing hype around starting lineups and promotional clothing fueled the movie star–like status of top players. Dad and Scott both expected good players to be humble. Good players had strong fundamentals, knew the game, and understood their role. Better players also understood their teammates' roles. And the best players developed basketball sense—they could see the entire floor and anticipate how the plays would unfold.

While Dad and Scott analyzed college basketball, Scott and I analyzed the high school game. A dozen years past our own games, we saw changes happening there as well. The high school game had also increased in intensity, and not all the kids were willing to work on fundamentals. By the end of the '90s, it was not enough to play the game for the joy and lessons it could provide. Some parents and coaches had raised the bar, with a state championship being the goal. Once a town had any team in their school make it to state, everyone knew it was possible for them as well. Why not shoot for the stars?!

We saw it happen in Dodgeville. After the 1993 trip to state, not getting there in '94 was a disappointment, yet one redeemed with another state appearance in '95. The kids who were in middle school during those years saw what was possible and their parents did, too. Some of those parents wanted their own children to experience that joy and glory. Some coaches also wanted it, and many were pressured by a new narrative for success.

Practices were stretched to the length and frequency limits allowed by the Wisconsin Interscholastic Athletic Association. *Because more is better.*

Kids started playing year-round. *They have to if they want a chance to make the team in high school.*

There were fewer three-sport athletes. *Specialization—that's the key to success!*

They were coached in the off-season. *If my kid plays on an AAU team, she could get a college scholarship.*

They started to suffer chronic injuries and more acute injuries. *Getting hurt is part of the game.*

These messages were reinforced among parents and coaches until beliefs became truths and very few people questioned them anymore. Instead of being a dream, there was an expectation kids should excel and go to state. This new reality of kids' sports felt very wrong to me and Scott. It was not what we'd learned as young athletes.

A coach in the making

As the oldest of five kids, Scott became independent at a young age. Both his parents worked full-time, his dad often on the second shift. At home they were often busy with his younger siblings. He spent a lot of time playing with boys in the neighborhood.

Throughout elementary school Scott and his best friend ran to their homes at lunchtime, gobbled down their food, and raced back to school to get a ball for recess. During the long winters of fourth and fifth grade, one of the teachers coordinated noon hour basketball games for the three sections of each grade. The boys played. We girls cheered. The goal was to keep us occupied in the small gym. Just a bunch of kids having fun. No parents. No expectations.

Though his dad had excelled in football, basketball, and baseball, he never pressured Scott to do the same. They watched games on TV occasionally, but their lives didn't revolve around sports schedules. He put up a basketball hoop on the garage for the kids to shoot at, and Scott's best friend had a hoop inside his father's large garage. Spontaneous games broke out between bike rides and trips to the swimming pool.

All that running home for lunch in elementary school made Scott a pretty good sprinter. When he was in sixth grade, the track coach invited him to compete on the seventh-grade track team. In seventh and eighth grade he enjoyed flag football because it was organized and new compared to the tackle games he and the other boys had played in their backyards.

Scott realized he had inherited some of his dad's natural athletic ability, so when he was placed on the third string of the basketball team, it rubbed him the wrong way. The coach was well aware he had potential but saw that Scott needed to figure out a few things for himself, like that working hard in practice is what gets you a starting position—which he earned by the fourth game. And rather than pull him out before it happened, his coach let him foul out of one of his first games and simply said, "You're going to have to learn you can't play like that."

Scott listened and learned. In high school he excelled at football, basketball, and track, earning the senior year award for outstanding male athlete in our class. Like my brothers, he enjoyed sports more than the classroom and did well enough academically to stay eligible to play. But when he decided on a college he became a more serious student. On the advice of our high school guidance counselor, he went to the University of Wisconsin-La Crosse where he could earn a degree in exercise and sports science in a program recognized for excellence.

Scott became certified to teach K–12, with a major in physical education and a minor in health. He also earned a concentration in coaching, which included two classes he was particularly interested in: the treatment and prevention of sports injuries and basketball theory. He was exposed to different basketball systems with a variety of offenses and defenses and plays for special situations. He began to look at sports through a different lens.

When Scott became a head coach, it didn't take him long to appreciate a message he'd learned in his psychology of sport class: *You will often want to win more than your players. Try not to take things personally.* The fourteen- to eighteen-year-olds he coached were busy with homework, dating, responsibilities at home or on the family farm, and jobs. Like Scott, many of them played three sports, most at least two. Sports added value to their lives; sports was not their life.

Scott's primary goal was to teach kids something, whether it was about the game, or life, or to stay motivated in school. He knew he couldn't reach every kid but wanted to reach as many as possible. Coaches make better connections with some kids than with others, as is true in every type of human relationship. At work and in sports, everyone has a role on their team. And every leader has a style shaped by their own experiences and their own coaches.

Scott was fortunate to play for or work with several successful coaches, each highly organized, each with a unique style. One emphasized strategy. One used psychology to motivate his players. Another could just as easily joke with and encourage his players as chew them out when he knew they could do better.

Scott became a little bit of each of them.

Coaching basketball players

I was always proud that my husband was a teacher and coach, but as a former player and mother of two little girls, I was thrilled when Scott transitioned to coaching the varsity girls' basketball team. Our daughters would have high school role models. The girls on the team would benefit from Scott's knowledge and love of the game. And from the bleachers, I would observe the progress and changes twenty years after my team got the chance to play.

The stigma and curiosity that had surrounded my high school team playing a "boy's sport" in the '70s was gone. There was no need for the girls to circulate a petition to get the opportunity to play. However, though no one laughed at girls playing basketball, the Dodgeville program had struggled in the shadow of a top-notch volleyball program led by varsity coach and our friend, Julie Van Epps. Her teams made two trips to state and won the championship both times.

Like Scott, Julie was a disciplinarian and a shrewd strategist. Her winning teams were built on strong fundamental skills. We were thrilled when she agreed to be his JV/assistant coach. She knew the girls and believed in Scott's approach. She helped bridge the gap between him and his players until they believed in him as well. Until they believed they could win at basketball, too.

I was eager to support the team and excited to see how the girls' game and skills had improved over the twenty years since I'd played. But it wasn't just the game that had changed.

My team had worn cutoff shorts and old t-shirts for practice. This team had practice uniforms. We had kept our hair pulled out of our eyes in a simple ponytail. This team's pregame routine included curling irons and makeup, and a few added color or sparkles to their hair. A player occasionally arrived late to practice because she'd squeezed in a tanning appointment after school. Many of them were on low-fat diets, despite their coaches' encouragement to fuel their bodies for sport.

Most of the girls also played volleyball, but there were a couple who thrived on the game of basketball. Scott had a talented farm girl on his team who, like some of my high school teammates, was expected to—and wanted to—contribute to her family's farming operation. She was allowed to participate in one sport; her choice was basketball. Another girl reminded me of myself. She was very focused on wanting to play basketball and learned everything she could about the game.

Slowly, the girls began to believe in Scott's program, and for every parent who disagreed with his vocal coaching style, there were two cheering him on, saying it was what the girls needed. The girls began to understand that Scott knew the game, knew how to help them improve their skills, and knew how to out-coach the opponent's coach for a win.

There was a special place in my heart for all of the girls on his teams. There was so much for them to learn, and he enjoyed teaching them. He knew they had potential and pushed them to do their best. To learn the fundamentals and strategy of the game and to have fun playing. I knew that every single day they were learning something about themselves, whether they knew it or not.

His coaching style clicked with most of the girls, but not all. And a few parents definitely took issue with his approach. One night after a long day of teaching and coaching, followed by playing board games and reading to Lauren and Kylee before bedtime, Scott collapsed in his recliner and gave me a funny look.

"I had a mom chew my ass out today. She said I'm too hard on the girls, and she doesn't like my coaching style. She went off for several minutes. I just listened—let her get it all out. I told her I understood that she's looking out for her daughter, but my job is to look out for the team."

I listened carefully and nodded.

"I said, 'Look—I'm coaching basketball players. I coach the girls the way I coached the boys. I want them to learn and understand the game. I care about all of them. If I yell, it's to try to light a fire under them—I want them to care, too. If I'm not getting after your kid, then I've stopped caring.'"

I nodded again. I knew why Scott thought that way. And I knew why the mom thought the way she did. But it seemed more complicated than coaching boys or coaching girls. It's impossible to coach any two *people* the same way and get the same results. I'd learned that from my experience in the Aquin game. And I knew that girls were more likely than boys to bring their friendships and personal conflicts into the gym with them. I had learned that from surviving junior high and playing sports with girls.

Players also react differently on an individual level to male and female coaches. When Julie Van Epps coached volleyball, she was tough, had high expectations, and didn't hesitate to chew a player out. But when Scott coached the same girls the same way, a few girls and parents found it less acceptable.

I could see the issues but couldn't offer assistance on how to deal with them. And I knew when our own daughters began playing sports, we'd have yet another perspective on the question.

A few years later, I read Kathleen DeBoer's book *Gender and Competition: How Men and Women Approach Work and Play Differently.* DeBoer provided insights into the complexities of coaching, for men coaching women or women coaching women. The dynamics were complicated when the book was published in 2004, and they've become more complicated by the new definitions of success developed over the last two decades.

But in the late '90s Scott did the best he knew at the time, and he believed in the girls until they believed in themselves.

Never give up

The morning of the big game we never expected to find our-selves in, I gave Scott some space, keeping our daughters occupied so he could mentally prepare for his team's toughest opponent of the season.

"How come we're playing this afternoon and not at night?" Lauren asked.

"This is a special tournament. You know how the girls haven't won many games this year? Well, today it doesn't matter. Today is a special game. The team that loses is done for the season. But the winner gets to play again *and* they get a trophy—they will be the regional champions."

I knew they *could* win. So did Scott. The question was whether the girls believed they could. The 1996–97 season had been long and difficult. Going into the regional, their record was 2–18. It had been heartbreaking to see them work so hard only to lose time after time, usually by just a few points. It wasn't for lack of talent or dedication.

Life isn't fair, Christine.

Many a night I found Scott in the living room at two a.m., questioning his coaching and wondering what he could do dif-ferently. They were good kids who worked hard and deserved to win. He was proud they had kept a good attitude through a very rough season.

And now we were in the post-season state tournament, when every team had a clean slate. We had gotten a bye in the first round of the regional, despite our record, and faced Iowa-Grant in the second. Early in the season, one of our two victories had been over Iowa-Grant, but they had beaten us just a few days prior in the last game of the regular season. In our third encounter of the season, on their home floor in what would be one of the teams' last games of the year, we were down 24–21 at halftime. But in the pivotal third quarter, our defense held them to just two points while we scored fifteen. We went on to win by ten, earning our way into the regional final.

*

I awoke that morning with a sense of excitement and anticipation. We were playing for the regional championship! Why *not* believe they could win? We had won only three games all year, and Royall had won eighteen, but I knew we were better than our record indicated. The win over Iowa-Grant had boosted the girls' confidence. We were the underdogs and had nothing to lose.

Any team can win on any given night.

As game time drew near, I got an overwhelming sense that something special was going to happen. We wished Scott good luck with hugs and kisses when he left for the game. We headed to the game a little later, the girls dressed in their Dodger game clothes: black leggings, Dodgeville Girls' Basketball t-shirts, and black and orange bead necklaces and hair scrunchies.

There weren't many people at the game. The season had been so dismal, only the faithful parents and a few fans even knew we were playing. My optimism waned by the end of the first quarter when we found ourselves down 16–2. The girls were obviously nervous and intimidated by their opponent. Scott helped them refocus, and I felt hopeful again as they hustled on defense and scored twenty points in the second quarter.

At halftime we were only down by six. Lauren and Kylee danced as the host school's band played, and I sent every positive message I could toward the locker room where Scott implored his team to not give up—to take it at 'em with relentless pressure.

The girls played as asked and were down by just four heading into the final quarter. They were playing better than I'd seen them all year. They were playing with confidence. Something special was unfolding. They weren't playing not to lose. *They were playing to win.* The crowd sensed it too and we cheered them on.

The girls played tough defense, and our team's leader, Melissa, outscored their leader 13–7. We were up by two points with forty seconds to go and I feared we would go into overtime. Then Melissa hit a three-pointer to put us up by five. I kept one eye on the game clock, the other on the floor, as Royall brought the ball up the court. We got a steal on a bad pass and protected the ball. I jumped up and down as the clock wound down.

When the buzzer signaled the end of the game, I couldn't stop the tears in my eyes from rolling down my cheeks.

"Why are you crying, Mom? We won!" Lauren said.

There was no way to explain to a seven-year-old that this was about so much more than a trophy. Melissa scored a career high thirty-four points, but it took every one of the girls on the team to win that game. I loved them for their perseverance. For believing in Scott. But mostly for believing in themselves.

I couldn't help but think of the poem Mr. Kaiser had given us that guided me through my playing days:

It's All In A State Of Mind

If you think you are beaten, you are;
If you think you dare not, you don't.
If you like to win, but you think you can't,
It's almost a cinch that you won't.

If you think you'll lose, you've lost;
For out in this world we find
Success begins with a fellow's will
It's all in the state of mind.

For many a race is lost
Ere ever a step is run;
And many a coward fails
Ere ever his work's begun.

Think big and your deeds will grow.
Think small and you'll fall behind.
Think that you can and you will;
It's all in the state of mind.

If you think you're outclassed, you are;
You've got to think high to rise.
You've got to be sure of yourself before
You can ever win the prize.

Life's battles don't always go
To the stronger or faster man;
But sooner or later the person who wins
Is the one who thinks he can!

— Inspired by 'Thinking'
by Walter D. Wintle

Ditto for a woman.

A new game plan

In the summer of 2000, at his retirement picnic, the athletic director whose shoes Scott was about to step into told me to kiss my husband goodbye. I assured him I knew what Scott was taking on as my dad had filled the same role. The reality was, it wouldn't be easy for any of us. I promised myself I would not let Scott's new job have a negative impact on our home life, our relationship, or the girls' well-being.

After seventeen years of coaching, Scott was ready for a new challenge, and knew he could apply his knowledge and passion for sports to the position of athletic director. Lauren was ten and Kylee almost seven when he took the job, and for a while we were able to set aside time on the weekends to do something fun together, but soon the job swallowed him whole. He was at school for fourteen or fifteen hours four or five days a week.

Wednesday was designated church night; several churches in town held religious education classes, so no games were scheduled. Instead, Scott attended school board meetings to report on athletics or facilities, or athletic booster meetings to discuss equipment needs they could assist with. Some games were scheduled on Saturdays, so he worked many of them as well. Sunday was usually a day off he could count on, but there wasn't much left of him at that point. At the end of each season, he attended every sports banquet, which consumed another two or three weekends.

Despite my best intentions, visits to our families became less frequent. I focused on the girls' activities and running our household, being the anchor of our ship, just like Mom had been.

Unlike the basketball season, athletic director duties are

year-round and almost 24-7: Parents expected his presence at a game, meeting, or event. A parent or coach had a grievance to discuss. Games had to be scheduled—and rescheduled when the weather got bad. Referees needed to be hired. Workers had to be present to sell tickets and keep the scorebook and clock. Someone needed to open the gym for weekend use, and he was the first point of contact. It was a thankless job, but he did it for the kids. And, in a parallel universe, the pay-for-play elite team movement gained momentum and complicated his job further.

In one unfortunate incident, some parents refused to return a gym key they had obtained legitimately for one-time use. They felt as taxpayers they should be able to access the gym as they pleased. But a public school district must serve all community members with no preferential treatment for talented kids or last names. They did not appreciate Scott's efforts to retrieve the key. This family, who'd been our friends in the early days of his coaching career, never spoke to us again.

Parents who invested many years in youth sports exerted pressure on high school coaches as well, expecting the return on their investment to be playing time for their child and a winning team. And a coach's time commitment grew way beyond the season, as they monitored their athletes' out-of-season activity and maximized the allowed out-of-season contact days. The excessive expectations and demands on their time and impact on their families made it harder to find people willing to coach the high school teams.

*

While our girls were in elementary and middle school, we encouraged them to try several sports and extracurriculars, to find two or three activities they could enjoy through high school. I'd read several books about raising daughters and tuned in to the growing number of news stories about overbooked kids racing from one after-school event to another. Kids across the country participated in more activities and started earlier than previous generations. Teachers and doctors reported that kids were overtired. I kept a watchful eye on the number of the girls' commitments, which required them to make choices and helped me see what they really cared about.

Even more concerning were the stories about youth sport injuries. Kids were playing organized sports early—before and as their muscles and bones developed. Doctors reported injuries never before seen in young children. They noted that many kids no longer moved their bodies through a variety of activities each day, from playing in their backyards and climbing trees to walking to school. Many injuries were caused by overuse—too much activity and too little rest—exacerbated when kids focused on a single sport.

Given the growing practice of kids playing a sport year-round and often two sports at the same time, we established a house rule for Lauren and Kylee: one sport per season. Just the idea of having to make that decision was crazy to me. *I'd been lucky to play at all.*

We had a public health issue in the making. *Surely parents would take heed and monitor their kids' activities.*

No one warned me to kiss my idea of youth sports goodbye.

SPORTS PARENTS

It's a girl!
When we were expecting our first baby, I worried that he would want to play football. Having grown up with brothers, I assumed that my children would be boys. And it seemed most boys wanted to play football. Scott had even played a year in college. But my fear started brewing when my brother was seriously injured as a high school player.

Dan was a junior when he broke his neck at football practice. It was my first fall out of college, and I was working in Indianapolis when my parents called to let me know he was having surgery at St. Anthony's Hospital in Rockford. I drove up to see him but wasn't ready for what I saw. He was suspended horizontally in the Stryker table, which allowed the nurses to rotate him. He spent half the time looking at the ceiling, the other half at the floor. His head was stabilized by a metal halo, secured with two bolts in his forehead and two more in the back of his head.

The surgeon fused bone from his lower back to repair his

neck. The bone that saved my brother's life was the width of a toothpick. A few weeks later he graduated to a halo that allowed him to sit, walk, and return to school. I think of him in that Stryker table every time an athlete is immobilized and taken off the field on a stretcher. I hate to see any injury during a game. And I certainly didn't want my own child to get hurt. Scott assured me if we had a boy who wanted to play football, he could be a kicker.

My worries disappeared as my pregnancy progressed because I had an undeniable sense that our baby was going to be a girl. When the doctor confirmed it upon Lauren's arrival, I thought, *Of course she is.* When Kylee was born two-and-a-half years later, I joked that having two little girls was my reward for growing up with three brothers. And having not had a sister of my own, I hoped that they would always support each other and be lifelong friends.

Scott and I were embarking on a special journey, raising girls in a new generation. Many of the doors that had been closed to Mom and me would be open to our daughters, but they would need resilience and confidence to walk through them. We agreed to support their interests and encourage them to be true to themselves. We would foster the talents and experiences they were drawn to. I owed that to my mother and grandmothers, and all the women we came from.

As my daughters grew up, I was grateful for the female role models in their lives—from the girls who played for Scott, to their teachers at school and the moms of their friends. And I was grateful for the female role models becoming more visible on television and in sports. My girls would grow up in a world where they would see women playing sports and assume it had never been any different. But for me, seeing women compete at the highest level was one of the most moving experiences of my life.

The power of the dream

The mail carrier placed the oversized green and gold envelope in our box at ten a.m. I opened it to find a small booklet and six bright gold tickets. We'd hoped for eight, but I was thrilled with what we received. When Scott pulled into the driveway that afternoon, I met him as he got out of the car, waving the colorful tickets. "We're going to the Olympics!"

When we learned the 1996 Olympics were going to be in Atlanta, we made plans to stay with relatives, who lived north of the city. We took our chances with the lottery system and requested tickets for four very popular events: the semifinal and medal games for men's and women's basketball.

It was fun to see the NBA superstars play in the semifinal game, but for me, the main event was the women's basketball gold medal game. On the morning of August 4, I triple-checked that the tickets were in my purse, reflecting for a moment on the significance of where I was headed.

I am going to see women play basketball in an Olympic gold medal game.

I hummed the Olympic anthem Celine Dion had sung at the opening ceremony: "The Power of the Dream." Women's basketball had debuted in the Olympics in 1976—the same year Lena-Winslow High School first offered girls' basketball. My basketball camp "friend" Lusia Harris was on that team. The Soviet Union won the gold in 1976 and 1980, when women's basketball in the United States was in its infancy, and coaches like Pat Summitt and Tara VanDerveer were laying the foundation for the future of US women's basketball. The USA had won the gold medal in 1984 and 1988. As our bus dropped us off within walking distance of the Georgia Dome, I was hopeful we'd avenge a 1992 bronze medal finish.

Twenty years after I learned how to run a 1-3-1 offense in our junior high gym on a cold dark winter evening, I stood in 103-degree heat and high humidity waiting for the doors to the Georgia Dome to open. The crowd of hundreds grew to thousands. Some held umbrellas or handheld fans that sprayed water. Despite the stifling heat, the crowd buzzed with excitement. The red, white, and blue clothing of US fans wove a colorful tapestry with the bright green and gold of Brazil as fans from both sides exchanged cheers.

"U-S-A! U-S-A!"

"BRA-ZIL! BRA-ZIL!"

Finally, the doors to the air-conditioned arena opened and we found our seats. As the teams warmed up, fans of both countries danced to the Macarena. I soaked up the scene vowing to never forget the day I was surrounded by thirty-three thousand women's basketball fans. Blocks of fans waving Brazil's flag. Blocks of fans chanting "U-S-A! U-S-A!"

Bright light focused on the court below us as the teams warmed up. Just before introductions, both teams went to the locker rooms for final instructions.

The lump in my throat grew as the announcer introduced each of the players for both teams. Goosebumps covered my arms. I couldn't stop the trickle of tears down my face as the women stood reverently for their national anthems. I thought about all the hours these women had put into developing skills and learning the game. All the obstacles they'd encountered as they pursued their dream to play basketball.

While the USA men's dream team had put on a show that highlighted individuals, the women executed fundamentals and teamwork with precision. They defeated Brazil 111–87. I cried once more as they took their place on the podium and received their gold medals.

Indeed. The power of the dream.

Just three months prior, on April 24, 1996, the NBA board of governors had approved the concept of a women's national basketball association. In October of '96 Sheryl Swoopes was the first player signed by the WNBA. Sheryl, Lisa Leslie, and many more to follow would become role models for girls across the country. In 1997 the league began playing, twenty-five years after the passage of Title IX.

Yes—things would be different for my daughters. They would be able to watch women play basketball on television. They wouldn't know a school year when middle and high school girls weren't playing basketball. And when she was in elementary school, Lauren found a college player role model just forty miles down the road.

On, Wisconsin!

In the winter of 1996, we took the girls to a Wisconsin Badgers Women's Basketball game at the University of Wisconsin–Madison Field House. It was the first collegiate women's event any of us attended. Lauren was six and Kylee was four. Scott and I were almost thirty-five. The women on both teams had skills that so far surpassed those of my high school team, I was as enthralled as my young daughters.

Having only ever been in a small high school gym, the girls took in the scene, their eyes as wide and bright as the gym floor. We sat just a few rows up from the end line under the Badgers' basket, watching closely as they warmed up. Lauren set her gaze on number 44 and asked me what her name was. We consulted the program: Barb Franke. At the beginning of the third quarter, Lauren turned to me and said, "I want to be like her when I play."

When we got home, we hung the team poster on Lauren's bedroom closet door.

A new generation

On a fall morning in 1998, I read the notice on the last page of our local newspaper: "Needed—Youth Basketball Coaches for City Recreation League." I could hear the thump-thump, thump-thump-thump-thump of basketballs striking the hardwood.

"Hmm . . . they need basketball coaches for third- and fourth-grade girls. If Lauren's interested in attending, I might as well volunteer."

Scott lowered his newspaper enough to cast me a questioning look. His eyes said, *I know there's no stopping you when you have your mind set on something*, while his voice asked, "Are you sure you want to do that?"

As an elementary PE teacher at the time, my husband knew exactly what I was getting myself into, and after eleven years of marriage, he knew a gym full of kids could be challenging for me. I'm an introvert who will choose lunch with one friend over a party any day. Though I truly wanted to volunteer, I took Tylenol *before* my friend and I led twenty girls in Brownie

Girl Scout meetings, anticipating a headache from their happy noise. But this was different. This was basketball. Low-stakes basketball. Just the fun of introducing them to the game.

"Sure, I'd love to teach them fundamentals. It's really important they know the basics and that's what I know best. It will be fun!"

I called the number in the ad to volunteer and two weeks later began teaching little girls the basics of dribbling, passing, and shooting, just as I'd been taught. Despite the early Saturday morning time slot, fifteen girls showed up, and I enjoyed getting to know them, especially the ones who had no experience at all with basketball and were eager to learn. They reminded me of my Lena-Winslow High School teammates learning the game as teenagers. I knew that for some of the girls, basketball could be a confidence booster and provide structure and support they may have lacked in their family or friendships.

Lauren was in third grade and excited about playing basketball, having spent every winter of her life cheering for the Dodgeville Dodgers while Scott coached. She thought it was pretty cool to have her dad as a gym teacher and her mom as a basketball coach. Two years later, when she moved up to the next age group, I had no qualms about continuing to work with the younger girls as Kylee was now in third grade. But Kylee was horrified the first morning when I grabbed my gym shoes and she realized I was not just dropping her off at the gym.

"How come you're going?"

"Because I love basketball. And I never got to play when I was your age. I want to help teach you and your friends."

"Have you ever done this before?" She looked skeptical. When Lauren was playing with the younger group and she and

I returned from the early gym sessions, Kylee would still be in bed. She was too young to realize what we were up to.

"I helped with Lauren's group, too. Don't worry, there will be some dads there. I won't be the only parent." *But, yeah, I'll probably be the only mom.*

I embarrassed Kylee long before she hit puberty, and her no-confidence vote registered loud and clear. I did my best to keep my distance once we got to the gym.

"Let's practice dribbling," I said to the twenty eager girls standing wide-eyed in front of me. I'd spread them out across the gym in four rows of five, giving them plenty of space to work with the ball and capture it before it interfered with others if it got away from them.

"Now, bend your knees, put your left leg slightly out in front of you, dribble with your right hand, and here's the hard part—look at me. Feel the ball; try to bounce the ball without looking down."

We practiced both bounce and chest passes. I showed them defensive position and had them slide across the gym with arms outstretched, hands up, ready to flip the ball away from the offensive player. But they wanted to shoot. *Doesn't everyone?*

"Put your fingers on the seam, bring the ball up in front of your face, keep your elbow in, and aim four inches above the rim. Bend your knees. Release the ball as you come up. Follow through reaching for the rim. Then follow your shot." *Just like Dad taught me.*

But it was way too much for eight- and nine-year-olds to take in. Some of the girls just wanted to throw the ball at the hoop, but most of them really wanted to learn. Following

Scott's advice from two years earlier, I broke the instruction into pieces.

Kylee was friendlier on the way home. "Mom, where did you learn all that stuff about basketball?"

"Well, Grandpa is a coach, and Dad is a coach, and I played the game, so I do know a little bit about basketball."

"Mom—you know a LOT about basketball!"

A year later, I wouldn't be so sure. I thought I was well prepared to be a sports parent. But everything I knew and valued was about to be turned on its head.

Mother knows best

The day the mother of Lauren's classmate called to ask if she could join the elite team, I knew it was time to walk our talk. Scott and I had observed the change in youth sports for a decade, but now the issue would affect us personally. Participating would condone the practice of overbooked kids and dual loyalties to teams. Declining would make it public that we weren't on board. Participating would give Lauren credibility with her team. Declining would threaten her chances of being accepted as a serious player.

The day the coach called she seemed as sure that playing for the elite team would be good for my daughter as I was sure that it would not. She shared that Lauren had said she wanted to be on the team, but hadn't told us because she knew we didn't want her to play.

I would have struggled with our decision more if Lauren had lived and breathed basketball the way I had. I may have even convinced myself participating was the right thing to do. But this daughter of mine (*me*—the one who got out of bed and ran sprints and dribbled in her driveway almost every morning, all summer long in anticipation of basketball season) was more likely to be climbing the tree in the backyard or reading a book than shooting baskets.

Scott and I had been excited to get a hoop secondhand for the driveway. I'd imagined family games of H-O-R-S-E and two-on-two, but the girls weren't interested. I thought their classmates would come over after school to shoot baskets, but they didn't. I thought Lauren would spend time in the driveway perfecting her skills, but she wasn't so inclined. She was as athletic and competitive as Scott, but I didn't see the level of *desire* playing for an elite team would require.

Most importantly, we were raising a young woman, not a basketball player.

"No, thank you. We have to pass," I told the coach.

"Are you sure?"

There are two ways to play the game. I wasn't going to play *not to lose.* I was taking the long view for my daughter. I was *playing to win.*

"Yes, I'm sure."

Desire

When she was eight months old, Kylee spotted her recently washed blankie in the laundry basket on the living room floor. As she brought herself to her knees and leaned across the basket, I anticipated something video-worthy, so I grabbed the camera and began recording. Holding the basket, she came to a stand and made several attempts to lift her leg above the edge of the oblong basket until the weight of her little body tilted her forward and she found herself half in and half out. She rested a moment before a final lunge took her fully in, tummy down on top of the clothes. She wriggled around until she sat upright, snuggled her blankie to her chest, and sucked her thumb with a satisfied look on her face. On the recording you can hear my uncontrollable laughter. But you can't hear my pride. *My baby girl was determined!*

As soon as she was able, Kylee would twist and wiggle away from me as I tried to change her diaper. I often had to finish the process as she came to her knees on the changing table where she looked out the window and squealed at the birds. When she could walk, she'd chase them across the yard. When they flew off just as she reached out to touch them, her joyous face would fall with disappointment. But she kept on trying.

At the age of three Kylee pushed the dining room chair to the kitchen cabinets and crawled up on the counter to search the cupboards for snacks. At four she insisted on choosing her outfit for the day.

She could be very independent. But she also watched Lauren carefully. If Lauren did it, Kylee did it. If Lauren had one, Kylee wanted one, too.

Sometimes it made sense for them to have or do the same things. But as my girls' personalities developed, a story my aunt Carol had told me was stuck on replay in the back of my mind. As a fifth grader Carol had been very excited to be in the class of one of Mom's former, and favorite, teachers. Until the teacher asked if she was as smart as her sister, and she knew she would be compared to Mom the entire school year.

I was determined to foster Kylee's unique interests, her own identity. She was not a replica of her sister. So, despite our lack of enthusiasm for soccer, when Kylee wanted to play, we signed her up. The cold fall morning my eight-year-old took a soccer ball in the face, I thought sure she'd be done, but she was undeterred. She had *desire* to play soccer. Real desire comes from within. It can't be taught. And it can't be faked.

*

When my brothers and my family gather at our childhood home, too much food and just enough wine ensure that we linger at the table over conversation. From politics to education to music, we share our views without judgment. Often someone resurrects a childhood memory that leaves us laughing till tears roll down our faces. After one Thanksgiving dinner my sister-in-law dared to ask the obvious question: Why did we all play basketball but not the piano?

It was the same question I'd asked myself many times. Did I love basketball because Dad did? But if I, a fourteen-year-old introvert, hadn't truly wanted to play, would I have gotten out on the court? The piano was as important to Mom as basketball was to Dad. Why didn't I play basketball *and* the piano?

It wasn't as though I hadn't tried.

I remember sitting at the piano with Mom when we lived in Palatine, the red primer on the stand, plunking out a short melody with my right hand. But the left hand was more difficult, and when I tried to combine the two, I got frustrated, cried, and quit. Until I decided to try again. It was a routine repeated over several years. I wasn't willing to put in the time to master the basics. I was lousy at counting time. And I preferred to hunt and peck, picking out a familiar melody of a popular song.

I lacked desire. The desire that motivates each of us to pursue what fills us with joy.

Lauren asked as a second grader when she could start piano lessons, so I called around to find a teacher to get her started. Two years later, when there was an opening, Kylee took the lesson time before Lauren's on Fridays after school. She wanted to learn to play like Lauren and Grandma.

At first Kylee practiced enthusiastically, but over the next few years, I saw a distinct difference in my daughters' approaches. Lauren practiced diligently every night after supper to get the timing right and polish an assigned piece. Something beyond wanting to get out of washing dishes motivated her. But during five years of lessons, Kylee had to be reminded to practice and she raced through her pieces; they were chores to complete, not food for her soul.

Like me, she preferred to play popular pieces by ear, and she played well enough for her own enjoyment, but I sensed she played out of obligation. When I discovered that a local artist offered children's painting classes in her home, I suggested she do that instead.

When my two daughters sat at the kiddie table in our living room with crayons, coloring books, and blank paper, Kylee had been the one to work laboriously. She took note of colors and details at an early age. When she was in kindergarten, we could pick her drawings out from her classmates' because unlike most of the stick figures with basic facial features, Kylee's people had eyelashes, earrings, and fingernail polish. She was as happy going to art class as Lauren was going to piano lessons.

It *was* a shame I didn't learn to play piano. But Mom never forced me. Never signed me up for lessons with someone else and insist I play. Never stood over me while I practiced. She understood that *wanting* to do something and having *desire* are two different things. And now I'd had the opportunity to recognize the difference with my own daughters.

Kylee learned the choices we make when we are true to ourselves feel a lot better than making choices to please others. She continued to enjoy the piano, on her own time and own terms. And she continued private art classes through high school, inspired by her teacher/mentor, someone meant to be part of her life. Kylee also found the confidence to speak up for herself. And I learned to listen carefully when she did. Her desire was more important than mine, even when it came to my favorite sport a few years later.

*

At the end of her freshman year, Kylee wanted to talk about her three high school sports experiences. I can imagine how difficult it was for her to come to her decision and break the news to me.

"Mom, would you be upset if I don't play basketball?"

"Of course not. I had a feeling . . . You aren't enjoying it, are you? You shouldn't play if you aren't having fun."

"I know, but if I don't play, I'll be letting a lot of people down. You, Dad, and Lauren, my grandpas, and most of my aunts and uncles all played. And I'm tall so everyone thinks I should play," Kylee said.

"Those are not good reasons to play. We all love you for who you are, not because you play basketball. The season is too long and demanding if you don't want to be there."

Insisting a daughter play through a long sports season when she didn't want to would certainly invite some kind of trouble.

The decision to play or not was hers to make. Unlike joining an elite team, the commitment to play for her school team rested solely on her shoulders. The financial cost was minimal, and the choice of where to spend her time and energy was hers. The high school years provide kids space to make their own choices, and what they learn from the outcomes will guide them in bigger decisions. I trusted there were several factors that led her to this point and knew months of careful weighing had brought her to this decision.

Talking about the situation years later confirmed that was the case. As a freshman she had assessed the situation and decided it wasn't for her. The expectation to play year-round would take time away from volleyball and soccer, which she had enjoyed more than basketball. She had picked up on the parental politics that had trickled down to the girls. Her closest friends were dropping out. And—it just wasn't fun. After looking forward to playing four years of basketball, year one was such a bad experience, she chose to say "no" to my favorite sport, and I had to support her.

*

The following winter held the first basketball season in twenty-three years that I didn't have someone I loved sitting on the Dodgeville bench. But given the youth sports culture that had developed, I realized I didn't care. And *that's* what left a hole in my heart.

Pay to play

During her sophomore year, with no basketball to fill the winter, Kylee wanted to give club volleyball a try. I thought about the travel, the expense, and my reservations about elite teams; I still wasn't convinced they were as beneficial as organizers claimed. But I knew the club would keep her active through the winter and could provide the chance to improve her skills. And there was no conflict of interest with a school sport. When she agreed to pay a portion of the fee and uniform cost, I agreed to drive her to practice until she got her driver's license.

The club team Kylee was assigned to included girls from three or four area high schools. I imagined them coming together to play at a different level (I falsely assumed those on club teams were the more talented or motivated girls) and forming a bond (the way my Le-Win team had done). I'm sure that happens with some club teams. Unfortunately, not with the teams Kylee played on for two years.

I watched their games and wondered why a few of them were there. Because their high school coaches encouraged it? Because their parents wanted them to be busy in the off-season? It didn't seem to be out of desire to play the game. They put forth minimal effort and did little to get to know their team-mates on or off the court. The only indication they were on the same team was their expensive matching clothing. The teams didn't have any chemistry, and it didn't develop over the season. I was disappointed but not surprised.

Kylee developed friendships with a couple of the girls. And she got playing time with the opportunity to work on her skills. But she never described tournament days as fun. Neither did I.

Sitting in the bleachers, I had plenty of time to observe the youth sports industrial complex during the all-day tour-naments. Part of me wanted to be proven wrong about my assumptions. But I was taken aback the first time I entered one of the huge venues built specifically to accommodate a few dozen teams. It was a far cry from the Brands Park scene where Dad and the boys from his neighborhood met and organized their own games. These games were organized and scheduled by adults and coached by parents or young women not much older than the players. These players arrived with coolers, parents, and nice warm-up jackets.

Tournament days were long. We left the house by five-thirty or six a.m. and returned twelve to fourteen hours later. While Kylee played, I did my best to stay interested, but there was no feeling of school spirit, and with few friendships formed between the players the atmosphere felt very methodical and more like practice.

Some of the parents watched quietly like me, supporting our daughters with our presence. Others coached from the sidelines, conferred with their daughters between matches, and expected improvement and results for their investment. Playing club ball was their ticket to a starting position on their school team the next year. Some dreamed of a college scholarship.

I passed the time during one of Kylee's team's breaks calculating how much money was involved in the one-day tournament. Uniforms, warm-ups, shoes, food, drinks, gasoline, entry fees, team participation fees, overpriced junk food, and lousy sandwiches at the concession stand. There were people reaping bigger benefits from club sports than most of the girls ever would. And over the next decade more facilities would be built specifically to accommodate youth sports tournaments.

All in the name of doing what's best for kids.

Team dinners

Parental involvement in recreational and elite team sports seeped into high school sports in the early 2000s. One of the first signs was parents hosting the football team to gather for a feast the night before a game. Other sports parents loved their children just as much and soon these dinners were a matter of routine. A sign-up list was circulated at every sport's preseason player-parent-coaches meeting, so parents could choose a date to host the team. I certainly wasn't new to the idea of teams bonding over a meal. I was nine the first time Dad and Mom hosted one.

*

The smell of lasagna and garlic bread wound its way into the living room from the kitchen where Mom had spent her Saturday afternoon boiling noodles, cooking sauce, and slicing mozzarella cheese. Layer by layer she'd created a masterpiece in several pans that now filled our oven as well as the next-door neighbor's. The house was clean, and I had set the big table in the dining room at the front of the Victorian home we rented in Winslow. My brothers and I were on our best behavior, waiting eagerly for the first guest to arrive.

To emphasize the importance of playing good defense, at the beginning of the season Dad had promised his team a lasagna dinner at our home if they held an opponent to under forty points. The night they'd achieved their goal, one of the boys quickly reminded Dad of the deal, and Mom began calculating how many pans it would take to feed a dozen hungry teenage boys.

My brothers and I watched quietly and wide-eyed as the boys arrived and took their places at the table. Our only encounter with them had been watching them play from our perch in the bleachers. They seemed much bigger and older up close. Over dinner they alternately raved about the lasagna and told stories about their hunting or farming experiences. Dad told them about the dirt courts he played on at Brands Park and how he learned to drive at Lane Tech on the figure-eight track behind the school.

Over spumoni ice cream there was a lot of good-natured ribbing. Even a nine-year-old could tell the team members liked each other. Through the course of the season, practice by practice, game by game, they had developed something special. Respect. Trust. Team chemistry. I was sorry when the last boy thanked Mom and Dad and the door closed as he headed home.

Mom's lasagna became legendary, and in the years the team didn't meet the challenge, Dad found another reason to celebrate the season with them. It was a night everyone looked forward to.

I was happy to imitate my parents' tradition when Scott coached. Every year we invited his teams to our home for mostaccioli about halfway through the season on a Saturday night. They, too, were social evenings filled with camaraderie and a chance to gather off the court. As preschoolers, Lauren and Kylee were excited for the "Dodger Boys" to come to our house, and a few years later they were thrilled to host their role models on the girls' teams.

So it was with great anticipation that I planned our turn to host Lauren's team for the first time. I spent the night before the team dinner making two big pans of mostaccioli, and I left work early the next day to bake them while I prepared salad and bread.

Team dinners were scheduled on weeknights after practice, usually the evening prior to a game, with the assumption that we'd provide a relaxed place for the girls to make connections that would carry over to game night. That was my best estimation of the goal, anyway.

I envisioned the girls talking and laughing, enjoying a couple of hours together away from school and responsibilities. But that's not what happened.

The team rushed into our house from practice loud and full of energy. They filled their plates and ate quickly. There were random comments about a class, a teacher, or something funny that happened at school that day. Many of them had another extracurricular activity that evening. Once one girl announced she had to go, the others followed suit. They thanked me, gathered their belongings, and headed out.

There and gone in under an hour. I wondered why I'd gone to so much trouble. I sighed as I loaded the dishwasher.

They don't even know what they're missing.

*

I'd hoped it would be different with Kylee's teams—with different girls, different dynamics—but it wasn't. Yet, a decade later Kylee assured me that team dinners were indeed great bonding opportunities, and she has great memories of hanging out with her soccer and volleyball teammates.

Perhaps our team dinners fell on crazy homework nights.

Or perhaps we parents don't always see the reality of our children's experiences.

But sometimes, we see them quite clearly.

Stuck in the middle

Long before my daughters got to high school, I began thinking about how to help them navigate those difficult teen years when kids are trying to figure out who they are, and who their friends are. I read several books about raising daughters, including *Queen Bees and Wannabes,* the Rosalind Wiseman book that served as the basis for the movie *Mean Girls.* I was hoping to find a magic answer, or learn that girls had found a way to be kind to each other on their way to adulthood.

At the same time, I came across articles about the fairly new phenomenon of overbooked kids. Kids whose after-school and summer schedules were packed with everything from sports camps and other day-camps to music and art workshops. Like most kids, our daughters would have agreed to try almost any experience. It was up to us as parents to determine how much they could handle at one time. And to be aware of how well the adults providing those activities interacted with kids.

Then I came across *Just Let the Kids Play: How to Stop Other Adults from Ruining Your Child's Fun and Success in Youth Sports*, by Bob Bigelow, Tom Moroney, and Linda Hall. The authors addressed many of the concerns that had been percolating in my head about youth sports.

What I learned about these three topics: middle school girls, overbooked kids, and parental involvement in sports, coupled with my own middle school experience and time playing basketball, made it clear that we were in the eye of a hurricane. As Lauren headed into middle school sports, I hoped to learn how to help both my daughters survive the storm.

Despite knowing the difficulties, thanks to Scott and Dad, for school coaches in having large middle school teams, I liked the philosophy of our conference's middle school athletics: anyone who wanted to play could. Anyone willing to learn the game and practice her skills had the opportunity to be involved. The coaches placed kids on A and B teams according to skill levels so they could develop and learn the game from where they were. Kids on the B team were not cut from the team as they might have been if there was just one team of twelve to fifteen. Kids develop at different rates, and it didn't seem right to eliminate anyone that early. And they got the chance to see if they enjoyed the sport.

On paper, this sounds great, but there is a flipside. Middle school girls often make choices based on what their friends do. I knew that some of them went out for sports to socialize, rather than because they wanted to learn to play basketball. So, I could also see the coaches' point of view. When you're trying to teach skills and how to play a game, it helps when the kids really want to learn.

Lauren's first middle school volleyball season went as well as could be expected. But the presence of the elite team we had said "no" to had an immediate impact on the school basketball team. From my seat in the bleachers, I watched the social divide on Lauren's middle school team grow. Some of the girls on the elite team wore their special team warm-ups to the games. A few voiced their boredom while sitting on the bench, rather than supporting their school teammates during middle school games. They ignored two of the girls I'd coached in the city rec program—the same two girls whose excitement and desire had impressed me just one year earlier. The girls that with support may have become pretty good ball players. The girls who had tumultuous family situations and may have benefited greatly from participating in sports. They lost interest and dropped out.

I could not reconcile what I was observing with my own history of playing. Watching things unfold over the next two years confirmed for both Scott and me that we'd made the right decision for our daughter in keeping her off the elite team. By the end of eighth grade, Lauren had developed a solid group of friends with interests as varied as her own. But I still hoped that high school basketball would be different—that the girls might gel as one team.

So I was relieved and encouraged when Lauren was invited to join her classmates at a team camp in June the summer before they started high school. I had no greater aspirations than her making the team and enjoying a high school experience. I was hopeful that there were still some fundamental values and lessons of sport my daughters could benefit from.

There were. And they were going to learn them in the hardest possible way.

RESILIENCE

CHALLENGES

Three dreaded letters

A baby-blue surgical cap covered Lauren's blonde head. When she rose at home at four a.m. that morning, she had showered and washed her hair. We didn't know the next time she'd be able to and had no idea how difficult the daily task would become. She had also followed the prescriptive instructions for knee surgery by scrubbing her leg with antiseptic soap. Then she tossed on shorts, a t-shirt, and slip-on sandals as our pre-op nurse had advised, to keep things simple for the ride home.

Now, as she lay under a mound of white blankets to keep her warm, only her head and her hand with the IV needle visible, I felt her fear rise in my chest, passed through the invisible umbilical cord that forever connects a mother to her child.

Tears welled up in her blue eyes when the nurse came to wheel her down the hall to surgery. One escaped, trickling down her face. "Bye, Mom. Love you."

I brushed the tear away and kissed her damp cheek. "See you in a little bit. I'll be right here when you get back. I love you."

Scott leaned down and kissed the crown of her head. "Love you. See you in a while, Pumpkin Head." The name our delivery room nurse had dubbed her was still a term of endearment fourteen years later.

We knew the outcome of surgery would impact her health and physical abilities for the rest of her life. We wanted her to have a shot at going back to sports if that's what she wanted. But we really just wanted her to be able to walk normally—something I hadn't seen her do for weeks—and to run around and play with her own kids someday.

The lump in my burning throat grew, and I blinked back tears as Scott and I walked to the waiting room. I did a quick scan, debating where to sit. Chairs were grouped so several loved ones could sit together. Scott cleared his throat and told me he was going to run some errands. Having been married to the man for seventeen years, I knew better than to tell him he should stay. He would have gone crazy sitting in the waiting room all morning. He needed to make some of that time pass quickly with other distractions.

But not me. Even if one of us hadn't been required to stay, I wouldn't have gone anywhere. To leave was to invite trouble. I wanted to be as close to my daughter as possible.

I found what looked to be the most comfortable chair, settled in, and took a deep breath. My seat provided a clear view of the nondescript clock, a gold square with circles where numbers ought to be and hands pointing to ten after eight. Perhaps I'd hear something around eleven.

The earth-toned furniture looked new, and I detected the smell of new carpet and fresh paint. The shades of rust and green reminded me it was almost fall, which was a bit of a surprise, but then we'd lost our summer. Artwork intended to comfort me had been strategically placed on the walls but couldn't hold my attention. I picked up a magazine and flipped through the glossy pages, unable to find a story to capture my interest.

I focused on the fountain in the corner. Water spilled from the top copper tray to the next one situated slightly below it. And then to the next tray below it. And the next, and the next, forming a chain. I followed the water's path until it reached the base to be recycled, just like the question on a never-ending loop between my head and heart: *How could the sport I'd loved my whole life have caused my daughter so much pain?*

*

The day Lauren headed to basketball camp prompted fond memories of my two camps. The girls I met, the skills I practiced, but most of all the enthusiasm it sparked for my next season. As her days at camp passed, I hoped Lauren was having a similar experience, as well as bonding with her soon-to-be high school teammates.

All of those hopes evaporated when my phone rang on the last evening of camp.

"Mom . . . I hurt my knee." I could hear the tears in Lauren's voice.

Smashing my flip phone against my ear to hear her over the adjacent conversations on the third base sideline, I got up from the lawn chair where I'd been watching Kylee's team play softball and walked toward the open field behind us, a knot forming in my stomach.

"You hurt your knee? What happened?"

"I don't know for sure. . . . I jumped up for a rebound, and I think I landed funny or something. It hurts a lot, and it's pretty swollen. I think it's something bad, Mom."

The knot tightened.

"Is someone taking care of you?"

"Yeah, well, they gave me some ice for tonight. I'm just going to try to keep off it."

"Okay. Dad can leave early tomorrow morning and get there before camp ends. We'll get you to the doctor as soon as we can."

I wanted to be there, to hug and reassure her, but all I could do was say, "I love you. See you tomorrow."

"Okay. Love you, too. Bye."

Clutching my phone in my trembling hand, I felt a little nauseous as I walked back to tell Scott. *She hurt her knee! She hurt her knee!*

Scott had hurt his knee playing football and Dad had torn his Achilles tendon showing a boy how to shoot a jump shot. But I never anticipated Lauren would experience anything worse than the couple of sprained ankles she'd suffered in middle school. The hours crawled by through a restless night as I tried to quiet my worried brain. It seemed days had passed by the time she and Scott pulled into the driveway the next afternoon. I barely saw her face as she limped through the door of our kitchen. All I could see was her knee. The words gushed out before I could stop them.

"Oh, Lauren—what did you do?"

I stared at the cantaloupe in the middle of her leg.

"I'm sorry, Mom."

I hugged her as tears ran down our faces. I wasn't mad. I was scared.

*

I closed my eyes and listened to the water in the fountain. We'd made informed decisions and had been careful. When Lauren sprained her ankle in middle school, she mastered the crutches we kept handy in the storage room, and we made sure she was fully healed before returning to play. After the second sprain she wore ankle braces for volleyball and basketball. When she experienced several months of patella-femoral syndrome— pain in her knees likely caused by growing quickly—she wore a sleeve and limited her activity.

So, this time, why had she gotten hurt?

Part of the reason we'd said no to the elite team was to avoid overuse injuries. Lauren certainly didn't get hurt from overdoing it. I began to question our decision—did she get hurt because she didn't play enough? Was her body not conditioned enough to endure the intensity at which kids played basketball today? Were her muscles not developed enough? Not strong enough? I considered every angle, looking for where to place blame. It didn't seem fair if our efforts to keep her life balanced were partially to blame for her injury.

Life isn't fair, Christine, I heard Dad's voice remind me.

*

In the last game, on the last night of camp, after being taunted on her entry to the game by the opponent who would guard her, Lauren's competitiveness had kicked in. She was determined to beat her any way she could, especially on defense. She felt triumphant as she snared a rebound away from her, in the split second before she crumpled to the ground.

She described it as though it had happened in slow motion. "As I landed, my knee felt like it was ripped out of my body, pulled to the right side of the court, and then pulled back in. She took the ball away from me, everyone ran down to the other end, and I was on the floor. I didn't want to touch my knee because it hurt so bad. It felt like if I moved any part of my body, it would make it worse."

An athletic trainer gave her some ice. Her coach checked on her briefly, and she limped back to the dorm when her team was done for the night. The floor supervisor checked on her, but other than her childhood friend Ann, no one seemed too concerned. When Scott picked her up, the athletic trainer who'd seen her when it happened wasn't there; the one on duty didn't know what had happened.

Thankfully, Scott was able to get her an appointment the next day with a sports medicine physician after he called the athletic trainer from University of Wisconsin-Health who worked with our school. He watched as the doctor performed the Lachman test. He positioned Lauren's knee with a slight bend, then holding her thigh with one hand, gently pulled her lower leg forward. It moved forward, but not enough to indicate a torn anterior cruciate ligament (ACL). Then he stabilized the outside of her ankle with one hand and pushed the inside of her knee outward to check her lateral collateral ligament (LCL). Finally, he checked her medial collateral ligament (MCL) by stabilizing the inside of her ankle and pushing the outside of her knee inward.

"Well, I can't confirm that she's torn anything. I *don't think* she has. However, there's so much swelling it could be interfering with what I'm seeing. Let's get an MRI so we can be sure."

Scott drove her back for the MRI a couple days later. He tried to reassure her with the story we hoped would be true.

"It's a good thing he didn't confirm an ACL tear," he said. "That's about the worst injury you can get. You might have sprained a ligament, or it could be a torn meniscus—that's the 'cushion' in your knee. I did that a few years ago. They just trim a little of it off; it didn't take me long to heal."

We tried to keep a normal routine over the next few days as we waited to hear something. It was a Thursday, just after nine a.m., when the nurse called with Lauren's MRI results.

"Her ACL is gone," the nurse said. "We'd like to schedule an appointment with one of our surgeons." The words swirled in my head. My heart was thumping in my ears; I thought maybe I'd misunderstood.

"What?!" I stared at the phone on the kitchen counter and pressed the receiver to my ear, hoping Lauren couldn't hear me. "What do you mean?"

"Lauren's ACL is completely detached. The MRI shows a clean tear. I can schedule an appointment for you to meet with one of our surgeons next week."

In her efficiency to finish the next task on her list—*Schedule appointment for Lauren Hawkinson*—she offered no sign of sympathy or understanding. No indication she understood that the news that was routine for her was a bombshell for us.

"Ummm . . . uhh . . . ok . . . When do you want us to come in?"

I trusted my hand to write down the details my head couldn't process. *ACL. ACL. ACL.* The three letters pounded in time with my heart.

I hung up the phone and stared at my notes. *No. No. No.* It can't be. Collegiate football players and NBA players tore their ACLs, not fourteen-year-old girls playing games at basketball camp. How could I tell Lauren? Surgery! Rehab?! She's just starting high school! My mind raced. I needed some time.

Scott was working at the high school that morning, taking care of summer tasks in his role as athletic director. He was much better than me when it came to injuries. I needed him to help me break the news.

Lauren's eyes filled with tears, and her lips quivered as Scott told her about the MRI results. "But you didn't think I tore it! The testing was negative! The doctor didn't think I tore it!"

Kylee entered the room with a smile that disappeared when she saw our faces. Our eleven-year-old gently lowered her rear onto my knee and put her arm around my back.

"What's wrong?"

"Lauren's knee is hurt worse than we thought. She tore a really important ligament, the one that holds your knee in place."

We all sat together a while, processing.

"Am I going to have to have surgery?"

"Yes. They want us to meet with a surgeon next week."

"I'm not going to be able to play volleyball, am I?"

The news sank in slowly. We all knew that was a given. She probably wouldn't be playing basketball either. I pushed that thought out of my mind as quickly as it entered. None of us was ready to acknowledge that. Throughout the day questions bubbled up that none of us had answers for. The next day, as the initial shock wore off, my practical side kicked in.

Knowledge is power. I compiled a list of questions for the doctor. It was the only thing I could do to get a little control over the situation, over the nonstop voice in my head that needed answers. Why was her knee so swollen? How soon could she have surgery? What would it entail? How long would it take? What would happen after that? Was it okay for her to be walking on it? My list grew over the next few days, but the big question I wanted the answer to was—*why* did this happen?

Moments into our meeting with Dr. Kaplan I was grateful he would be her surgeon. He spoke directly to Lauren as he asked how she'd gotten injured and how she'd felt and what she'd done in the days since it happened.

He examined her knee, then, using an anatomical knee model, he showed her how the anterior cruciate ligament runs diagonally in the middle of the knee. Its job is to keep the tibia and femur bones in place and provide stability to the knee.

I could see what had happened but not why.

"How could this happen to her?" I asked him. "She's only fourteen. It's not like she's playing college athletics."

"Unfortunately, I am seeing more and more of these injuries. Especially in girls. Girls tear their ACL five to eight times more often than boys. One of the factors is the difference in the way girls' bodies are made. Their center of gravity is lower than boys' so their knees take more impact. Another is biomechanics—how they move their bodies. And then there's the force of the impact itself. When she landed, her shoe probably stuck to the floor but her knee kept going."

With no way to know for sure, I had to accept that one or more of those uncontrollable factors was responsible.

"Lauren," Dr. Kaplan continued, "I'm going to make you a new ACL."

He drew on her leg with a marker as he explained where he'd

make incisions and described how he would recreate an ACL to stabilize her knee. Because her growth plates weren't closed, he wasn't able to use her patellar tendon, the most common way to reconstruct an ACL. There were two other options: a cadaver donation or Lauren's hamstring tissue. We thought her own tissue had a higher likelihood of success.

"The surgery will take about three hours. I'll see you a few days later, then a week later, then two weeks later, and several more times over the next eight to ten months. We'll get you started on physical therapy soon, and you'll continue until you're fully healed and released," Dr. Kaplan explained.

"So . . . I'm not going to be able to play basketball this year either?"

"I'm sorry, no. I don't rush my patients through this process. It's not going to be easy because you're going to start to feel really good in about four months, but we know the tissues won't be fully healed. If you go back too soon, there's a risk of tearing it again. I won't release you until you're healed and have done well with therapy, probably at the end of April."

Lauren's eyes filled with tears and she nodded.

"We need the swelling to go down in your knee before surgery, and our schedule is pretty full. It will be the end of August before we can schedule this, so until then I want you on crutches and in an ELS [extension lock splint] brace. Let's protect your knee for the next few weeks."

After answering all of our questions, he introduced us to the man who would fit Lauren in the brace she would wear every day for the next five months. The black and gray contraption strapped to her leg, running from her ankle up to mid-thigh, was set initially to prevent her knee from bending or moving in any direction.

The three of us rode home in silence, digesting what we'd learned. I wondered why this was happening to so many girls. Girls (and boys) didn't tear their ACLs when I played basketball in the 70s. *Something was wrong.* Could it have been prevented? *And why, oh why, did it happen to Lauren?*

She'd so looked forward to playing for the Dodgers in high school and now her first season was over before it had started.

In the weeks before her surgery, as I watched my daughter hobble around in a brace and on crutches, my sadness and disbelief morphed into anger.

Why did this happen?! We made good, safe decisions for her. She's a great kid and doesn't deserve this. Playing sports is supposed to be FUN!

Now, sitting in the hospital waiting room, I wasn't sure she'd be able to—or even want to—play when this ordeal was over. And I really didn't care. I just wanted my girl to be whole again.

Lauren and I had arrived at the beginning of high school on two very different paths. I was grateful for the chance to play and learn the game with my teammates. She'd already played basketball for eight years and had now suffered a major injury.

This was definitely not my game.

Time-out

My wandering mind led me to Dad's induction to the Illinois Basketball Coaches Association Hall of Fame the previous year. The ceremony had reminded me what was good about youth sports. Dad was inducted not for producing winning teams or a state championship but in the category "Friend of

Basketball." He was recognized for his dedication to the game and the impact he had on the kids he coached. The hotel ballroom had been full of coaches who understood the importance of fundamentals and the benefits of being on a team, regardless of your role. Coaches who recognized it is a great responsibility to be teachers of life as well as the game.

The event had renewed my hope that my daughters would reap some of the benefits of playing high school athletics, and I had looked forward to this month when I thought Lauren would begin high school volleyball. Now, we were on a different path, and I was trying to sort it all out. I wasn't going to find any answers before she came out of surgery, but I did find more questions.

Five decades had passed since Dad played on the dirt courts at Brands Park. Almost three decades had passed since my friends and I learned to play girl-to-girl defense. Only a few years had passed since parents started orchestrating their kids' lives. Overbooking their activities. Trying to get ahead. Of what, I'm still not sure. But this new way of parenting was escalating quickly, and we all felt its presence. Just like the Dodgeville fans worried they wouldn't have a seat for the big game, anxiety grew in parents about whether their kids would get a chance to play if they didn't start early and play often. *Can this possibly be good for the sport? More importantly, for the kids?*

High school athletic associations across the country were pressured to change rules about coach-player contact time during the summer to accommodate the influence of elite teams on high school sports. Camps like the one Lauren had attended brought in teams, not individuals. It was a backdoor way for coaches to get their teams playing time together in the summer without breaking Wisconsin Interscholastic Athletic Association rules. It was also a great moneymaker for camp organizers and facility owners. But it excluded a lot of kids. So was it *really* good for the game, or just for the *very* small percentage of players who had a shot at playing collegiate ball?

And what about the injuries? How many coaches and parents knew about the growing number of sports injuries? How many of them understood the need for kids' bodies to rest as well as exercise? About the benefits of variety in activity and the devastating effects of overuse injuries on young bodies? Who else was willing to encourage moderation? And why, even though we did, were we punished with Lauren's injury?

"Hawkinsons?" The nurse interrupted my thoughts as she scanned the waiting room for us, but I'd already jumped out of my chair and headed toward her, with Scott close behind.

She led us to the day-surgery suite just before they wheeled Lauren back into the room. Her leg was wrapped in white from toes to torso and her face was peaked from the anesthesia. She was disoriented, nauseous, and shaky, yet the nurse, whose shift was ending soon, ignored her concerns and immediately began preparations to send her home.

Thankfully, the nurse who took over told us to take our time. Lauren could stay into the evening if she wanted. We waited a couple hours for her to feel more stable. Then the nurse put the ELS brace on and encouraged her to take the hydrocodone regularly the first couple of days to stay ahead of the pain. She helped Lauren into a wheelchair, and I carried the goodie bag of information and supplies as we left the surgical floor. Scott brought the car to the hospital entrance, and we got her situated on the back seat with her leg elevated on a pillow.

She slept soundly as we took the familiar route home, unaware of the extent to which her experience would impact her life.

You can never rebound too much

The same day Lauren had arrived home injured from camp I received an acceptance letter from the graduate school at UW–Madison. I had reached my early forties having devoted over a decade to keeping our household running smoothly and providing support to Scott and the girls in their endeavors while working part-time. Most of the time I was fine with my role. But Scott spent most of his waking hours at school, and the girls were teens with new interests and friends. It was time for me to start a new chapter of my life. I'd learned from my early career experiences that doing what I thought I was supposed to was a mistake; doing what I was meant to would serve me far better. I wanted my next adventure to feel as right as being home with the girls.

Like Nancy Drew, I looked for clues to tell me who I was before I forgot. I spent a few weeks excavating old journals and reading the papers I'd saved from high school and college. I applied some of the girl-parenting tips I'd learned to memories of my preteen self to find common threads and some direction. I found the notebook Mom bought me when I was seven that held the poems I'd written while sitting in the old school desk at my bedroom window in Palatine. I found high school book reports and my term paper about sexism in children's books. I found notes from teachers encouraging me to keep writing and wondered why I hadn't.

I began researching master's degree programs that would guide me to a profession I'd enjoy and ended up right where

I belonged, in UW–Madison's Life Science Communications program. It allowed the flexibility to take courses geared to my thesis topic. I intended to research and write about a women's health issue. I didn't know my topic would be delivered to me via my daughter.

*

Lauren started high school one week post-surgery, and for the first time in her life she didn't want to go to school. It was an ordeal just to get there. Getting dressed and out the door to the car took twice the normal time. She was able to back into the front passenger side of the car and sit down, then rotate her torso to the left while I lifted her straight leg up and into the car. We did the same in reverse outside the high school doors, arriving early to avoid the buses dropping kids off. I gave her a hug and wished her good luck.

The next week I began my own classes. Two days a week I dropped the girls off at school and by a quarter after eight I was walking up Bascom Hill with the energy of a twenty-year-old. Like Cinderella at the ball, I escaped my parenting and household responsibilities for a few hours, attending class and studying until the clock on Library Mall struck two. I drove home, took a twenty-minute power nap, and turned into Mom again. On the other three days I worked part-time and took care of the household chores. Many evenings I drove the girls to piano or art class and attended their events. I hadn't had such a jam-packed schedule since my WIU Union Board days. And I thrived despite Lauren's situation weighing heavily on my mind.

Lauren was grateful for friends who carried her books and

opened doors for her and the teacher who gave her a seat in the front row so she could prop her leg up during class. But her knee throbbed and ached under the wrappings and brace, and she was terrified to walk in the hallways, afraid she'd get her crutches knocked out from under her. Every day was a struggle. I wondered how long it would take my daughter to find strength and motivation.

*

As the weeks progressed, we got proficient with the logistics for showering, dressing, and getting Lauren to school. She became adept at navigating the school halls on crutches and timed her departure from class so she could get to the next one before the halls filled with students. And she saw a physical therapist twice a week.

I encouraged her to think of her therapy sessions as "practice" that would get her back in the game. At least she had a visible record of her progress. At first she struggled to flex her knee, then slowly but surely gained mobility and function with each passing week. We celebrated when she could make a 90-degree bend, and she kept working toward the 120-degree goal.

By early October she could walk in the ELS brace without crutches, though Dr. Kaplan advised she keep using them in the school halls to create a safe space around her body. Her physical rehab was well underway. But her mental rehab had barely begun. She was missing her first season of high school volleyball, and she was frustrated by the girls on the team who were only out to stay in shape, and by all of them for taking the chance to play for granted.

She couldn't play volleyball, and she couldn't sit at the piano, so she had to take a break from lessons for a couple of months. She'd lost two of her anchors. I thought about the advice I'd received in college: *She needs five connections to feel like she belongs.* I was grateful she could play her clarinet in the band and that she had a great group of friends.

A tough third quarter

By November Dr. Kaplan gave Lauren the all-clear to stop using the ELS brace. *Finally! Things are going to feel normal again.* Then he explained that during the next few months her ACL was very susceptible to reinjury. Four months after an ACL repair, the capillaries begin to bring new blood flow. It's a rebuilding that occurs in phases, a vital but invisible healing process. She was at high risk for reinjury. The next few months would be tough for different reasons.

"I want to see you monthly now [instead of bimonthly] and your visits to the physical therapist will gradually taper off. If you plan to return to sports, you may want to consider our Performance Spectrum program at UW Health. You'll work with an athletic trainer to learn how to move your body and land properly. It is not uncommon to tear an ACL a second time, and learning proper mechanics can help prevent that from happening," Dr. Kaplan said.

I leaned forward in my seat. The thought of her tearing her ACL again scared the hell out of me. I couldn't imagine going through this a second time. I was eager to fast forward to a time where this injury wouldn't be the first thought behind anything she did. I wanted my kid to be able to walk the halls between class and not worry if someone was going to knock her over. To be able to dance at the school winter dance. I wasn't sure she'd want to play sports again, and I really didn't care.

I watched her face as Dr. Kaplan described the Performance Spectrum program, which met twice a week in the late afternoon, requiring that she miss the end of the school day. She set her jaw tight and barely spoke until we got in the car.

"I can't miss my class! I'll get behind! You and Dad are busy. I don't want you to have to take me to Madison. I'm not going!"

The schedule did pose some challenges, but a few days later Scott and I proposed a plan. Scott would drive Lauren halfway to Madison and I would meet them after attending class. I'd then drive back to Madison with Lauren while Scott went back to supervise games at school. We'd agreed to do this twice a week for the next four months. Lauren felt guilty about the hassle and because the program wasn't covered by insurance, but we insisted. When she rode with Scott, they listened to classic rock. She and I listened to her music and talked. And with our busy schedules, we all started to look forward to having that one-on-one time in the car.

*

When basketball season started, Lauren watched her team practice, and we all went to the games.

"I was able to do a few things. Coach Heibel was great. He let me do what I could to help out during practice, and I kept the book for the away games. I was able to be involved a little bit. But some of my teammates didn't understand," Lauren said.

Every time a teammate asked when she was going to join them on the court and she explained she would be doing rehab for four or five more months, the chasm between them grew.

They were moving forward with the season without her. Even her best friends had grown weary of injured Lauren. No one even noticed the first day she went to school without her brace; it had become invisible.

"Except for you guys and my athletic trainers, I felt a lot of the time that no one knew what I was going through or how I felt."

She liked her athletic trainers who worked with her in the Performance Spectrum program, and though she was tentative on her first attempts to jog or take small hops, she trusted them and slowly began to trust her knee. Soon, she was teaching her body how to come to a full stop before turning a corner. Occasionally, I'd watch through the window, studying her knee. *Was it turning in slightly? Did she take that corner too quickly?* But I too trusted the athletic trainer, who gave her his full attention, and unlike me, actually understood her body's mechanics. She was learning to move again. Safely.

The day she ran for the first time in six months, we celebrated like she was a toddler taking her first steps. And like a toddler, she had good days where she felt strong and confident and tough days when she was frustrated by the slow process.

One day while waiting for her session to begin, both of us wondering for the hundredth time why this happened, I said, "You know, sometimes things like this happen to people, and it sends them on a career path."

She snapped at me, "Well, not me. When I'm done with this, I don't ever want to be in a doctor's office again."

On the sidelines

One evening Lauren and I arrived at the gym after her rehab class just as the junior varsity game was ending. I headed to the same seat in the bleachers I'd sat in for the past fourteen years watching Dodgeville boys and girls play basketball. But now I was watching with new eyes.

As the band played "Stacey's Mom" I watched the visiting team warm up. They shuffled in a star pattern on their end of the court, barely stopping at the corners before switching directions. Two hours earlier I had watched the athletic trainer teach Lauren how to stop correctly and plant her feet solidly before turning her body to change directions. I was sure neither the coach nor the girls knew they were putting themselves at risk for injury by executing this drill so lazily.

An idea started to formulate. I wanted to know why Lauren tore her ACL, but I also wanted to know if coaches were aware of the drills she executed in Performance Spectrum—if they knew they could reduce their players' risk of injury by incorporating them into practice. When the second semester started, I took a class called "Health Care Issues for Individuals, Families, and Society." I discussed my ideas with my professor, who recognized kids' sports injuries as a public health issue and encouraged me to explore the topic through my thesis. Maybe I'd get some answers to my questions after all.

*

In the dark days of that winter, Lauren read, competed in forensics, and looked forward to auditioning for the spring play. Most importantly, she turned her attention back to the piano. She'd gotten out of doing dishes many a night by telling me it was time for her to practice, and now I was grateful there was *something* in her life that could bring her joy. Seated at the piano she could forget about her knee and the sports she was missing. She set a goal with her piano teacher to master a favorite but difficult piece. Night after night she worked on a section at a time, determined to achieve perfection in something she had control over.

Some nights things just didn't click, but most evenings the piano provided solace she couldn't find anywhere else. "Gabrielle's Theme," written by local surgeon Dr. Adam Dachman, became her signature piece. When our family gathered in Mom's living room and Lauren sat on the piano bench at Mom's Steinway, my brother Michael encouraged her to "Be the song."

She had found her strength and motivation. And in a parallel world, her perseverance in rehab was also rewarded.

Lauren saw Dr. Kaplan the day before her fifteenth birthday. He looked at her Biodex scores for muscle strength and endurance and noted seven months had passed since surgery. She wasn't supposed to be released till April, but when we told him she'd completed four months at Performance Spectrum, he said she was good to go. Lauren declared being released a month early the best birthday present ever!

We went out for lunch to celebrate how far she'd come. We weren't ready to think about how far there was yet to go.

PERSEVERANCE

Back in the game

After being cleared for activity on her birthday, Lauren began taking slow jogs, working up to a run. She played in a summer basketball league so she could ease herself back into activity. She was thrilled to join her teammates on the volleyball court in August, but the workouts were intense, and the conditioning part of practice was painful. She was afraid her teammates thought she was trying to get out of it, but the coaches were supportive and told her to listen when her body said to stop. She grew stronger, completed the season without incident, and looked forward to basketball, which started after a couple of weeks off between the two sports.

Three of Lauren's sophomore classmates were moved to varsity immediately, so she and the other sophomores formed a JV team with some of the freshmen. Her coach was a lot like Scott. He knew the game, embraced fundamentals, and some parents thought he was too tough on his players. We understood it was the kind of tough that meant he cared and wanted to help them improve. He also cared about them as kids first. He wanted to know the details of the rehab Lauren had been through the past year, and he checked in with her during practice to make sure she was okay. He encouraged a slow but steady return to the game and told her to take breaks when she needed to.

She had missed a whole year of skill development, but she and her teammates developed a camaraderie quickly. I was grateful to those girls and her coach for providing a safe and supportive team, but I had mixed emotions as the first game drew near.

A new season

I dropped Lauren off at the high school that morning before heading into Madison for class, expressing nothing but excitement and happiness for her. I tried to concentrate on my readings before class but couldn't shake the concern that if Lauren was overly cautious, she could get hurt again. I reminded myself that her body and muscle memory would take over. I had to trust that all that rehab, all those trips to Performance Spectrum would protect her.

There was just enough time that evening to review Kylee's homework and fix sandwiches before heading to the gym. Scott was already there working in his capacity as athletic director, and Kylee sat with me in the bleachers until her friends arrived. Sitting alone I scanned the familiar walls of the gym and remembered the boys of '93 and '95. I remembered the night Melissa hit a half-court shot for Scott's team to take the powerhouse Cuba City girls' team to overtime. Off to my right on the wall was the tribute plaque to our good friend and Scott's assistant coach, Julie Van Epps, who had passed after a long battle with cancer. She had asked us if we were going to let our girls play with the white ball, too. *You bet they are, Julie.*

Fifteen years had passed since I first sat in this bleacher seat with baby Lauren on my lap, and for the last couple years, I wasn't sure this moment would ever come. I blinked back tears as Lauren ran onto the court to warm up with her teammates for the first time. *Please let her play safe.*

It was good to see my daughter run up the court, but her attitude was serious rather than joyful, and she didn't have the spark she'd had in middle school. I watched her face as carefully as her knee, looking for any sign of distress. By the end of the fourth quarter, she started to relax, and as the clock wound down on their first win of the season, she smiled. When the final buzzer sounded, I allowed myself to exhale the breath I'd been holding all evening.

I watched her team head to the locker room, but she didn't look up at me. And instead of following her teammates through the door, she stopped in the hallway just off the gym. Her coach stopped, put his hand on her shoulder, and said something. She nodded and wiped her eyes. As he walked away, I hurried down the bleachers and into the hallway to give her a hug. She was shaking but fine, overwhelmed with the emotion of playing again.

"I'm okay, Mom. I'm okay."

A learning curve

The previous summer I took a six-week class about the sociology of sport, where we discussed the role of sports in society. The professor prompted us to think about sports in ways we never had before. On the micro-level we knew sports were about values and work ethic, skills and attitude, roles and teamwork. But on a macro-level sports had ethical, financial, political, and social impacts. Our class discussions made me think about who benefits from sport and how.

That fall, as Lauren returned to sports, I returned to the health sciences library where I pulled volumes of the *Journal of Athletic Training* and *Journal of Sports Medicine* off the shelf to scan the table of contents for topics relevant to my paper. I was encouraged that there were health care professionals concerned about the increase in ACL tears overall in young athletes and specifically the higher incidence in girls. Researchers examined everything from body mechanics to menstrual cycles to the composition of playing floors, looking for causal relationships. Was it genetics? Were some bodies predisposed to injury? Was it because the female body structure has a different center of gravity than males?

I learned that when males tear an ACL, it's often the result of a contact injury; female tears are usually non-contact, often occurring as Lauren's had when landing from a jump incorrectly or planting a foot and changing direction too quickly. I read every study that time allowed as I worked on the literature review for my thesis. It became clear there was no definitive answer. Lauren's injury was likely due to bad mechanics and bad luck.

One afternoon I found a study about the psychological impact of injuries. I found it interesting that, according to the authors, different genders react to injury differently. While boys focus immediately on working hard to get their bodies back to the sport and their team, girls need the social connection and have trouble feeling like part of their team. They need to be included and supported until they can return. I had observed what the authors described firsthand.

I finally understood why I had felt so lost when my appendectomy had ended my high school playing experience. The study also explained how Lauren felt when her teammates didn't understand what she'd been going through. Her injury had further widened the gap between her and the girls who'd played on the elite team. She had said that the hardest thing about her ACL journey was that her teammates and classmates didn't understand the seriousness of the injury.

The study also revealed that girls who have several hobbies and interests are more resilient than those who lose the one thing they focus on. Once again, I was grateful Lauren had friends and interests outside of sports. I knew in the long run she was going to be just fine. But what about all the other girls who play sports? I wondered what their coaches knew about injuries and eagerly began the qualitative research for my thesis.

During January and February of 2006, I interviewed twenty-one coaches and athletic directors at what I had categorized as small, medium, and large high schools. I probed their knowledge of youth sports injuries, injuries to girls, and prevention and rehabilitation of injuries, and their openness to learning and incorporating prevention in their practices. Most of them acknowledged they were woefully ignorant. Our conversations prompted a couple to take action. Only one coach, whose team had suffered numerous ACL tears, was already working with an athletic trainer to incorporate injury prevention into his team's workouts.

*

With my thesis defense scheduled for May 11, I buckled down in March to collate what I'd learned. Typing furiously, I realized there was much more I wanted to explore and much I didn't have time to include. I became overwhelmed and got so sick I lost a week of progress in April. I made a trip to the student mental health services offices where a counselor gave me some sage advice: Completion not perfection. I had to let some of it go. I promised myself I'd do something with it later.

As graduation neared, I explored the idea of becoming a communications specialist for the sports medicine team at our local hospital, hoping to raise awareness of youth sports injuries and continuing the conversations with coaches and athletic directors about injury prevention and rehabilitation. The director liked my ideas but simply didn't have a budget for such a position. I didn't have the luxury of waiting for a job doing what I would have loved to do and accepted a writing job with an electronic medical records software company a couple months later.

The transition from part-time work to full-time while parenting was the hardest of my entire life. It was the only time I wasn't excited and happy to embrace a change. In many respects I felt like my life was over. The "free time" I'd had to pursue my master's degree would be replaced with work hours. I only had time for two purposes for the next five years: work, and supporting my daughters through high school so they'd be ready for college.

Changes
Heading into her junior year, Lauren was ready to do some college visits. Though I could have seen her majoring in music

or library science, her strongest interests since middle school had been in history and archaeology. We visited Scott's alma mater, University of Wisconsin-La Crosse, where they had a strong archaeology program. It gave her something to think about during her most challenging and busiest school year yet.

After playing middle hitter for the volleyball team that fall, Lauren slowly gained confidence in her knee and began looking forward to playing varsity basketball. Her teammates were more skilled and more experienced, but she came in off the bench when needed and accepted her role on the team. We were all just glad to see her playing, though I was hyper aware that an injury could change everything for any of them in a split second.

When I wasn't thinking about injuries, I compared Lauren's playing experience to my own. Players' knowledge and the physical intensity of the game weren't the only things that had changed. Instead of cutoff shorts and old t-shirts, Lauren's team wore reversible practice jerseys provided by the school. I had worn low-cut canvas Pro-Ked sneakers. She wore Adidas high-tops made of leather and ankle braces for extra support for her often-sprained ankles.

We had the support of occasional volunteer cheerleaders at our games. Now, though there were designated basketball cheerleaders, they cheered sporadically for the girls' team and always for the boys' team. They made locker-grams for the boys but not the girls. Our high school band had played for us as they did for the boys. But the volunteer pep band only played occasionally for Lauren's team with fewer kids showing up than for boys' games, and even fewer staying for the second half.

We had been expected to ride the bus as a team to and

from games. Now, many parents signed their child out after the game and drove them home. I understood it allowed them to spend time with their child or to get them home faster to do homework. Or maybe it was just more convenient for the parent than driving back to town to pick her up at the school. But something was lost. We had ridden to our games in silence, focused on the game before us, but laughing or commiserating on the rides home was part of what made us a team.

Girls and boys continued to share limited gym space, alternating early and late practices based on game schedules. The girls still waited patiently for their time on the court and moved on slowly as the boys walked off. The boys still ran on and started shooting the moment the girls were done. And while the girls supported the boys at their games, only a handful of boys came to the girls' games. Some changes don't happen quickly enough.

*

Lauren played a supporting role on the talented varsity girls' team of 2006–2007, led by the girls who had played on the elite team. They made it to the sectional championship postseason, and while she was sad when they lost, she was not devastated. She kept the outcome in perspective as she put greater value on her friendships and qualifying for the state music finals by earning a perfect score on her piano solo at the regional solo and ensemble contest.

She also had bigger things on her mind. Despite her objections in the Performance Spectrum waiting room about a related career, during the winter she had decided to become an athletic trainer. A few months later she applied to four college programs. Then she focused on enjoying her senior year of classes and activities.

Lauren's final countdown

Lauren was determined to make the most of her senior year. She finally got to a place mentally where she could put her injury behind her. She played hard as a middle hitter on the volleyball team and carried her work ethic onto the basketball court.

After almost making it to State the year before, the girls drew more fans to their games. Expectations were high. They could get to the Kohl Center this year. Lauren's friends cheered her on, bringing a "We *heart* Lauren" sign to almost every game. After two years of playing tentatively, Lauren approached her senior year differently. She played like the Lauren we'd known in middle school. Though she had never put in the time to become an excellent shooter, she had a signature move under the basket that Scott had taught her. She came in off the bench and hustled, rebounded, and played good defense. She made such progress that year that she earned the most improved player award.

Mid-season, after an important win where she'd played several minutes, a longtime fan approached me after the game.

"Wow—your daughter played great tonight. I didn't know she had that in her!"

I smiled and nodded. I did.

I also knew she had it in her to do well when she chose to attend Winona State University to study athletic training. She had traveled a different path than me but had learned just as many valuable lessons from sports.

And Kylee traveled yet another path, learning lessons of her own.

A season from hell

When Kylee was little, I sometimes felt guilty that she didn't get the undivided attention a firstborn receives. But then I realized that when Lauren went to kindergarten, we would have a couple special years together. And when Lauren went to college, Kylee's high school activities were front and center on our calendar. I had gone back to work full-time when she was in eighth grade and appreciated the buzz of excitement on her game days. Driving from my out-of-town job to her soccer and volleyball games reminded me of when I was a young coach's wife, driving from work to Scott's games.

Once the weight of basketball was lifted from her shoulders, Kylee didn't look back. She played hard and loved soccer, especially in the rain and mud. In the back of our minds, we both knew she could get hurt like Lauren, but we didn't discuss it. Her best friends were on the team, and they played the game together with joy.

I observed the games quietly, sometimes chatting with another mom as Scott worked the home games, running the clock and scoreboard. I wish I had learned more about the rules of soccer, but I had difficulty staying engaged as the girls worked so hard for a chance to shoot the ball, often to be snagged by the other team's goalie. The game required a different mindset than basketball, one I had not developed.

But I learned to love volleyball, even though I hadn't even played it well in high school PE class. I had been a line judge for the Le-Win girls' team and could enjoy watching the game, watching my daughter use her power to jump, swing, and drive the ball down over the net. For a girl to feel that strength and power—that's a confidence-builder.

Kylee's junior year was filled with camaraderie as the volleyball team had some success. She liked her teammates, and they gelled as a team. Many of them were also soccer teammates so they met again in the spring on the soccer field. She anticipated a fun and fulfilling senior year.

Instead, she got one of the most challenging experiences of her life.

*

The summer before her senior year Kylee contracted mononucleosis. She spent the first three weeks of July on the sofa, her face tinged green and yellow, her eyes glassy and turned down at the sides of her face, with a look that wasn't at all my daughter's. She had been looking forward to volleyball season and had spent the weeks after the soccer season ended running and lifting weights on her own in preparation for her final year.

We were relieved when by mid-August she regained her energy and started taking easy runs around the block. She got the okay to play when practices started and left the house on her first morning of volleyball filled with anticipation.

She returned in tears.

She was one of three seniors and a junior who showed up for varsity practice that morning. The rest of the varsity players had bailed without warning, choosing to run for the cross-country team instead. Their betrayal shook her seventeen-year-old soul.

"WHAT the heck?!" she said through angry tears. "We just played in a tournament last weekend, and no one said anything about not coming out."

I didn't understand either. I knew some of the girls and parents had issues with the coach and guessed that was the primary reason for switching sports. Perhaps they had debated their decision all summer. Though it was clearly their choice, they certainly could have handled it better.

The coach had no choice but to move up inexperienced freshmen and sophomores. They did not have the skills for the varsity roles they were forced into. So, rather than perfecting an offense and honing skills, the four upperclassmen became encouraging teachers and mentors.

Kylee and her co-captain, Jess, supported each other through the frustration and disappointment. Some days it took everything Kylee had to be positive through practice; she barely made it into the house before breaking down in tears. She cried after every game the first half of the season. During evenings at home, she turned her attention to the more important tasks of her senior year. She was determined to earn an A in AP calculus, and she was submitting college applications. I felt helpless, able to offer nothing more than steadfast support. I had to trust there was a lesson in there somewhere.

As the season progressed, Kylee learned to celebrate the small stuff. A freshman who perfected her overhand serve. A sophomore who learned where to set the ball for Kylee to spike it to the other team. Successful volleys with the opponents, even if they didn't end in a point. A young teammate eager to learn who thanked her for advice.

She learned patience and team-building skills as she encouraged the younger girls. And their parents praised her positive attitude and leadership. It took courage to go out on the court, game after game, knowing there was a minute chance of winning.

They won two matches and lost twenty-nine that season.

Life isn't fair, Christine.

No one wants their child to have such an experience. And if winning was the only thing Scott and I valued in sport, we would have told her not to waste her time. It wasn't the senior year any of us anticipated, but most of life isn't what we anticipate. We don't get to choose our challenges, but we can certainly learn from them. Persevering through match after match, loss after loss, was difficult. But the maturity, self-respect, and self-confidence Kylee gained were the building blocks of resilience. Resilience she drew on in college. Resilience she needed when she was laid off nine months into her first job. I knew she would be fine. She'd learned how to rebound.

*

I am ashamed to say that I never learned the rules of soccer. Kylee says I was removed from it and I have to agree. Over twenty-three years I'd become disillusioned with high school sports, more than annoyed with parents inserting themselves in the game, and I questioned what it meant to be on a team. I didn't have the energy to do more than support her desire to play.

I appreciated soccer like I'd appreciated *Barney and Friends*, knowing it wasn't for me, but my daughter was having fun. I saw it in the way she looked forward to practice and games. I saw it when she played in the rain and mud. I saw the camaraderie and success she shared with her teammates. If we hadn't followed her lead, she would have missed her only positive high school sports experience.

Lessons for life

Through the bumps and turns of their high school sports experiences, both my daughters learned more than we realized at the time. In the end, they learned the same lessons I did. The same lessons Dad talked about. The lessons of sport and life: fundamentals are key to success; we have to embrace our role; and persevering through challenges builds resilience. But mostly, it has to be fun.

THE FAT LADY SINGS

Dad, the coach

Dad loved the skills and strategies of basketball, but for him coaching was about more than the game. It was about relationships. About the kids. Right from the very beginning.

As a young man starting his career in Palatine, Dad taught, coached, and worked many a recess duty. One day a fourth-grade boy named Chris asked him to throw him the football in the lot where the kids had recess amidst the teachers' parked cars. Dad took the ball, told him to run down to the Chevy and turn left at the Buick, then tossed him the ball. It became a daily routine for Dad and Chris. Three years later Chris tried out for Dad's seventh-grade basketball team. Even though his athletic ability favored football over basketball, he became a starter for Dad because what he lacked in ability, he made up for with effort and desire to improve.

In 2013, as retired adults, Chris and two of his classmates, grateful for lessons learned from Dad, paid him a visit. Chris had become a high school football head coach and won five state championships. Dave, who had been quite a good basketball player, had a successful career in sales. Dad remembered Roland as a great kid who was good friends with the boys who played basketball, so he came out for the team. Unfortunately, Dad had only twenty uniforms and had to cut Roland from the team in both seventh and eighth grade. Knowing how important it was for him to be part of the group, Dad asked him to be the team manager. Happy to have a role with the team, Roland thrived. He went on to be an educator and eventually an elementary school principal.

That these three men took the time to drive two hours and spend an afternoon laughing and reminiscing about their junior high experience with my father demonstrates the impact a coach can have on players.

We heard many stories over the years about kids who had played for Dad. He fostered special coach-player relationships with many of them, regardless of their talent or role on the team. He respected his role of coach for his players as much as his role of father to his children.

Dad, the father

Though he may have occasionally cued us on the driveway, reminding us to keep our elbow in while shooting, or to block out and rebound in a game of two-on-two, Dad never interfered with or commented on our high school sports teams. He understood the importance of us respecting the coach who led us and of being a good team member. He let us deal with the challenges and learn our own lessons.

My brothers had different experiences and have different memories than I do, but Michael's is particularly telling. He played high school sports after the rest of us had left home for college. Dad was retired and could have micromanaged Michael's sports experience. He did not. He knew the difference between coaching players and raising children.

Michael recalls, "The most noteworthy thing about my experience with Dad and basketball is that he never discussed Xs and Os with me. Not once. My friends and my friends' parents always assumed that Dad was constantly discussing the game with me. Probably because that's what they did. The only thing Dad ever said to me about playing basketball was 'Have fun.' He said this to me before I left the house for every game.

"No matter how well or how poorly I played, he never made any comment about my personal performance. He would sometimes remark about the turning points in a game, but he neither praised or scolded me for my individual performance. That's just the way it was.

"When we played at Pearl City my senior year, I probably played the worst game ever. Our coach benched the entire first string the whole second half. The second string came back from being about twenty points down and nearly won the game at the end. In the weeks that followed several people remarked to me that Dad was standing and clapping the entire second half. People pointed this out to me like they were shocked. They expected him to be upset that I had been benched. He never said a word to me about how bad my performance was.

"After I graduated, I was always taken aback when people who attended Lena-Winslow would ask me how Dad was and tell me some story about him. His former players almost all had some recollection of how playing for him was fun. This is the thing about Dad as a coach, he knew where the fine line was between taking the game seriously and having fun."

Dad continued to enjoy Le-Win sports in his retirement, often watching the children or grandchildren of the players he coached in the 1970s. He especially enjoyed watching junior high kids and was eager to share his observations about kids with potential when we visited.

"He could really be tough someday, if someone would just work with him."

"He has big feet and he's not coordinated yet, but he could do well in high school."

"If I could have an hour a day with him in the driveway, he could have a beautiful shot."

He saw kids that age as raw material; if they had the desire, he could teach them. So, a decade after his retirement, in 1997, he began coaching seventh graders. I think it was probably one of the most fun experiences of his entire career. For three years, he put all his effort into coaching those boys and sharing his wisdom. He loved to tell us how the kids were learning and when things clicked.

He was there to coach the boys about basketball, but he never missed an opportunity to teach them about life. One day as his team left the gym and began boarding the bus for an away game, a boy ran up to him with a panicked look on his face.

"Mr. Maher! I don't have my uniform. My mom forgot to pack it. What should I do?"

"Next time, pack your own uniform."

Applying lessons learned

If asked what I wanted for my children from sports, I'd say it boils down to that. And they did indeed learn how to pack their own uniforms. The greatest benefits they received from sports were to learn to follow their desire and to know they are resilient.

Six years into her career, Kylee bounced back from not just one, but two layoffs—a job hazard of working in the advertising industry. The most recent occurred the first week of the pandemic lockdowns and job postings mostly disappeared. With no job and nowhere to go, she returned to her paints and easel. Creating art for family members was an enjoyable way to pass the time, and the break allowed her to think about her next career step. By the time jobs began getting posted again, she had decided to change direction, and she landed a job with a talented in-house design team for a major health care organization.

Inspired by the athletic trainers who helped her return to sport, Lauren earned a master's degree in exercise and sport science. She treated and rehabilitated Division 1 athletes' injuries for eight years, working long hours and managing high stress situations before deciding to focus on her greatest interest, the prevention of athletic injuries. Research has shown we can prevent injuries. She is working on a PhD with a goal to broaden awareness and increase implementation of injury prevention programs.

I reaped the same benefits from sport as my daughters. It took me ten years to write this book, mostly an hour at a time. Sometimes I had to call time-out; sometimes I wasn't sure I wanted to continue. But desire kept pulling me back to my writing desk. And during the pandemic, I took the opportunity to make this book a reality, just like that fourteen-year-old girl going out on the court for the first time, her kneecaps shaking, but determined to play the game.

Women in sport

Women's sports have made great strides in the past fifty years. Girls can participate in high school sports without signing a petition and without being laughed at as they play. Women receive scholarships to play collegiate athletics. Women's college and professional basketball games are televised throughout their seasons.

And yet, there are still glaring inequities. Only four percent of sports media coverage is dedicated to women's sports. Upon the passing of Pat Summitt in 2016, Bill Plaschke of the *Los Angeles Times* admitted that as a prominent sports columnist for a prominent newspaper, he never in twenty years covered one of her games. He voiced his regret: "But to marginalize greatness because you don't think many people are watching is embarrassing, even shameful. Summitt's life showed, that when it comes to women's sports, if you follow the ratings, you miss the point."

In March of 2019 the US Women's Soccer team sued for discrimination in the areas of pay, game locations, travel and frequency, training, and medical treatment. The transgression prompted their fans to cheer "Equal pay! Equal pay!" when they won the World Cup later that year.

In April of 2019 when asked why she said she would never again hire a male assistant coach, Muffet McGraw, head coach of the highly successful women's basketball program at Notre

Dame, explained the inequity: "We've had a record number of women running for office and winning, and still we have 23% of the House and 25% of the Senate. I'm getting tired of the novelty of the first female governor of this state, the first female African American mayor of this city. When is it going to be the norm instead of the exception? How are these young women looking up and seeing someone that looks like them, preparing them for the future? We don't have enough female role models. We don't have enough visible female leaders. We don't have enough women in power. Girls are socialized to know that when they come out, gender rules are already set. Men run the world. Men have the power. Men make the decisions. . . . When you look at men's basketball, 99% of the jobs go to men. Why shouldn't 100 or 99% of the jobs in women's basketball go to women?"

Those are just a few of the big examples.

Inequities start when girls are young. The youth sports programs that many families take for granted are not available to many girls of color or girls from families with lower incomes. The Women's Sports Foundation, founded by Billie Jean King in 1974, helps communities get girls active and provides research, education, and advocacy with the goal to enable all girls to enjoy sports. They help girls and women achieve in sports and life so that they can be role models for the next generation. Role models that are needed. Because little girls are still watching from the bleachers.

One night when Lauren was at a men's and women's basketball doubleheader at the University of Richmond, where she worked as an athletic trainer, she texted me: "Taylor, Coach Eb's daughter, age 6, was sitting next to me during starting line-ups for the men's game. She goes, 'Why, why do they get so excited about the boys but not . . . but not the girls?' She sounded so offended when she asked. Like she thought everyone should be more excited about the girls than the boys."

I thought about Taylor when we attended a Minnesota Lynx game six months later. With Kylee working in Minneapolis, seeing a Lynx game was at the top of my visit to-do list. Twenty years after the Women's National Basketball Association began, twenty years after we saw the US women win the gold medal, I was going to see my first WNBA game in person.

As we wove our way from the top level of the full parking garage, down flights of stairs, and through covered walkways, we were surrounded by hundreds of excited fans—men, women, and kids of all ages—everyone decked out in fan gear. Their buzz carried us through the maze to the entrance of the Target Center. I listened as Lynx fans discussed how the team was doing, which player was struggling, and whether one would be okay and playing today after an injury.

There was no need to rush. We'd allowed plenty of time before the game, but the crowd's electricity created a sense of urgency. There was something special waiting for us inside. My pulse quickened. In the concourse we found the usual ball game eats—and kiosk after kiosk of fan gear. Hats, shirts, bandanas, signs, posters, glassware, and trinkets galore promoting the women's team. I wanted to buy a Lynx jersey, move to Minneapolis, and get season tickets.

The Lynx team included Lindsey Whalen, homegrown Minnesota talent who had played for the Golden Gophers at the University of Minnesota. And I was eager to watch Maya

Moore, who played for Geno Auriemma at women's basketball powerhouse University of Connecticut.

They were playing the Los Angeles Sparks, who had their own stars in MVP Nneka Ogwumike and Candace Parker, who had been recognized as Illinois High School Miss Basketball in 2003 at the same ceremony where Dad was inducted into the Basketball Coaches Hall of Fame.

We found the stairs leading to our seats on the top row of a short wall, reminding me of our reserved seats in the Le-Win gym where I'd watched Dad's teams play forty-five years earlier. Music blared for several minutes then stopped briefly as the announcer asked the fans to welcome their team to the court. The crowd of thirteen thousand roared. The atmosphere in the nearly full venue exploded with music, dancing, and cheering as the Lynx and Sparks warmed up on the court below. The home crowd created a sea of Lynx blues and greens. Many of their shirts proclaimed, "OUR HOUSE."

Tears filled my eyes. It was a sight I couldn't have dreamed of as a young girl. I wanted Taylor to know she could.

*

Four months later, Scott and I watched on TV as the same two teams battled for the WNBA championship. They traded games in the best of five series with the Sparks winning the first and third games. Game five was held in the Target Center where it was hard to pick out a yellow shirt amid the home team crowd.

Also on television that night, the Packers were playing the Bears. Scott checked their score occasionally. We also checked on the Cubs as they were making their way into the World

Series. But no one could argue the fact that the women's game was the most exciting sporting event on TV that night.

The next morning the Packers were on the front of the sports page, no surprise as we live in Wisconsin. The Cubs were on page three. I have no doubt had I been looking for the men's NBA championship results, there would have been a big story on the front page. But I scoured the sports section twice before I found a list of the WNBA scores for the championship series of games in small print. There was no article about the WNBA championship. No synopsis. No box scores. Just a final score: 77–76.

I was able to find the story in the Minneapolis *Star Tribune* online.

*

When women's teams fight for their rights, when women's coaches fight for what's right, and when sportswriters stop ignoring half of the good stories, they set good examples for the rest of us to question the status quo.

When my teammates and I stepped onto our high school basketball court, we prompted people to challenge their assumptions about what girls can or should do. Lessons I learned on the basketball court, and from my dad and husband, gave me a unique lens to watch the youth sports system evolve into one with such high expectations that it delivers fewer benefits to fewer children than we assume it does. My hope is to prompt people to challenge their assumptions about what youth sports can or should do.

Too much of a good thing

I have great respect for athletes who play collegiate, Olympic, and professional sports. I still enjoy watching teams who play with strong fundamentals and win with strategy. And I still love an upset.

I appreciate that some kids have the right combination of talent, desire, and athleticism to play at the highest levels.

But 97 percent of our children are never going to play in college.

When it comes to youth sports, I am pro opportunity for all and pro raising healthy kids. Too many children are victims of a system that burns them out before they can reap the real benefits of playing high school sports. Others are excluded for economic reasons. And many are eliminated for lack of talent before their bodies and interests have had a chance to develop.

I am inclined to think that in their hearts, most parents know this system should be different and many want it to be different. On the outside they may reinforce the belief for each other that sitting on the sidelines watching their child play all day is what good parents do:

> *Oh, she loves it! We all love it. It's so much fun to go to the games.*
>
> *It's so good for them to be in the gym—better than playing video games all day.*
>
> *They are learning so much. They will have such a good team in high school!*

But friends have confided:

He's burned out. You know . . . they started playing in second grade and he says it's just not fun anymore. He isn't going out for varsity.

When they were playing in the regional and hoping to get to state, he told me if they didn't make it, his whole life would have been wasted.

I don't really like the whole traveling team thing. We're on the run all the time, she doesn't always get to play, and it costs a lot. But if we don't, she won't even have a chance to play by the time she's in high school.

The last concern came from a family friend whose daughter was nine years old. Nine. The same age I was sitting in the bleachers wondering why the boys didn't just shoot at the closest basket. When her daughter was a sophomore in the early 2010s, it looked like their commitment had paid off. She started on the varsity team. We went to see her play, and she was pretty darn good. The next year we didn't see her name in the box score and worried she'd torn her ACL. We learned later she had stopped playing because she didn't enjoy it anymore.

In 2016, five years after my own children's high school sporting events ended, I was interested in my coworkers' take on youth sports and listened carefully when I heard them talk about their children's activities. One day a father groaned when I asked about his weekend plans.

"What am I doing? Sitting in a gym watching sixth-grade girls play basketball ALL day Saturday. Which is really just watching them chase a ball all over the court. I hate Saturdays."

A mom who had played high school basketball a decade

after me described her children's sports schedules: "It's too much. It's too much, and it makes kids think they're a lot more important than they are."

When we create state championships for sixth graders and giant posters of seniors to hang on the gym wall, what are kids supposed to think? Who is sending that message?

When I voiced my dismay to one sports father, he replied, "It's our society. We can't change it."

Well, society changed to get us to this point, didn't it?

*

Even in the late 90s, before the number of extracurriculars for kids exploded, I was a bit overwhelmed by the opportunities for my elementary-age daughters: Brownies, 4-H, dance, music lessons, art classes, gymnastics, soccer, softball, basketball, summer school enrichment programs. Before the term was even coined, I started to experience FOMO (fear of missing out). There were so many good things they could do!

But parenting magazines and columnists warned of the new phenomenon of overbooked kids and reminded parents that kids need rest, and they need time to be bored. I wanted my daughters to have time to play in the backyard or read a book. It wasn't hard for us to heed the advice when the girls were in elementary school, but I knew it would get harder as they got older. Especially when it came to sports.

In 2001, as I read the newly released *Just Let the Kids Play: How to Stop Other Adults from Ruining Your Child's Fun and Success in Youth Sports*, I was relieved that others shared our concerns. The authors provided observations and guidance on everything from organizing youth sports to physical and emotional injuries. And they implored parents to evaluate the system and make changes.

I was encouraged until I realized I was probably the only person in Dodgeville who read the book. Youth sports programs were still relatively new and perceived positively. Most parents were grateful their kids were busy for a couple of hours and happy they were getting exercise and learning the value of being on a team. My concerns about too much too soon would have been met with a polite smile and nod.

*

I am still trying to figure out why the youth sports craze escalated as quickly as it did, but there seems to have been several contributing factors. In the 1990s savvy marketers began targeting families with fewer children and greater disposable incomes than previous generations. They were ready to meet families' demands for everything from clothing to video games, from music to acting lessons, and of course, sports. Many parents had the financial means to provide experiences for their children that didn't even exist when they were kids. And many mothers began experiencing sport vicariously through their daughters the way men had with their sons for decades.

At the same time superstars like Magic Johnson, Larry Bird, and Michael Jordan opened the door for the NBA to rebrand itself as entertainment. Players appeared in commercials and movies. Kids could wear their favorite players' shoes and jerseys, and watch the superstars in dunk contests. Starting lineups became light and sound productions. The hype trickled down to college and then high school sports.

We felt so close to the action, it was easy to believe the

dream could come true for our kid, too. If they played early enough and put in the hours, maybe they could *Be like Mike.* And even if they couldn't, playing AAU ball could make them *feel* like Mike.

The Amateur Athletic Union (AAU) was founded in 1888 with the goal of creating common standards in amateur sport. For most of its first century AAU was the governing body for Olympic sports, and its teams and competitions highlighted elite athletes. In 1978 Congress passed the Amateur Sports Act, which decentralized the AAU and required separate oversight for every sport. The focus shifted from developing Olympians to developing youth sports programs.

AAU clubs were formed with sponsorship from shoe companies hoping the talent that emerged would promote their brand. And the marketers did a great job of convincing parents that their tournaments are the best places to showcase a child and for coaches to find the best players. The number of teams grew rapidly to accommodate the demand—to give any kid who wanted a shot to be able to play AAU ball.

If they were lucky, perhaps they would play for a coach who really knew the game. But high-profile players and coaches have criticized AAU ball for everything from lack of fundamentals to lack of respect for the game. The name and the investment provide the illusion that all kids who participate are good ball players. A very few are; the others are supporting cast members.

A very long and costly shot

The NCAA website provides the estimated probability of high school athletes competing in collegiate sports, with data for each sport. In 2018–2019, 540,769 boys and 399,067 girls played high school basketball, with 18,816 boys and 16,509 girls going on to play in college. That is 3.4 percent of boys playing basketball (1 percent to Division I, 1 percent to Division II, and 1.4 percent to Division III), and 4.2 percent of girls (1.3 percent to Division I, 1.2 to Division II, and 1.7 percent to Division III). So, about 5,400 boys and 5,187 girls (out of nearly one million players) across the country went on to play Division I basketball, where athletes are most likely to receive athletic scholarships.

Yet many parents are convinced that starting their kids early and spending a lot of time and money (for a decade or more) will surely lead to a scholarship.

In the 2019 article "Kids aren't playing enough sports. The culprit? Cost," ESPN writer Kelly Cohen highlights research the Aspen Institute initiated to understand why in 2018, only 38 percent of kids aged six to twelve played team sports on a regular basis, down from 45 percent a decade earlier. The survey indicated costs and inconvenience—and no surprise, kids were simply not having fun anymore.

There is no denying that the expense makes organized sports difficult if not impossible for many families. While costs vary based on the sport and equipment required (from $420 for cross-country to $2500 for ice hockey), the Aspen Institute study found the average amount of spending per child, per sport, per year to be almost $700.

The Aspen study also found that the average kid quits sports at age eleven.

I'd like to hope that some of the reason for the decline in early participation is because some parents are realizing that playing organized sports before the age of twelve is more likely to burn their child out than light a fire. Or maybe parents are recognizing the opportunity costs to their families and children. Over the course of ten years, the money spent chasing a dream could finance part of a degree. And if the additional playing expectations were eliminated, many a high school student could enjoy playing for their school, participate in other activities, work part-time, and graduate better prepared for college.

But what if your child *really is* destined for collegiate athletics? What if they have the desire, the talent, and the resilience it takes to play at that level?

If your child *is* one of the 3 percent, then you need to learn as much as you can about the recruiting process and how your child can prepare both physically and mentally for the experience, because any young athlete playing at the college level is going to need more than talent to succeed. And coaches may not be looking for what you think they are.

Thoughts from a college coach
In 2015 I interviewed Michael Shafer, then head coach of the Richmond Spiders Women's Basketball Team, who shared his insights on recruiting and youth sports.

What are the most important skills or characteristics you look for in recruits?
First of all, I'm recruiting students for the university. She has to be a good student to be successful in the classroom and earn a degree. Second, she has to be competitive. I'll take competitive over talent. If you're going to play, you have to want to win, knowing that you aren't always going to. Third, I look for kids who have played more than one sport—which is getting harder to find—and especially if

they've been on a winning team for any of the sports. That means they know what it takes to win and how hard they need to work.

What do you think motivates college players?

What we see today is that many players are skilled but have no motivation. The world shifted in the 1980s—we had to start rewarding kids to build self-esteem, and I think it backfired. Instead of protecting kids, I think it made them vulnerable. They need to build self-confidence through achievement. They think mistakes equal failure. So when something bad happens, they don't know how to deal with it.

Kids used to be motivated to play the sport and compete. Now many are playing to get a college scholarship because college is expensive. But by the time they get to college, and they are expected to play at a higher level, they don't want to do it anymore. They don't like it. They're not playing for the right reasons. They're not competitive, and it's not fun—which was the whole point to begin with.

You said you look for kids who've played several sports. Why not specialize?

My neighbor told me his ten-year-old is going to specialize. I said, In what? He's ten; he should specialize in being a kid. Otherwise he's going to burn out or get injured. The chances of getting a scholarship are about 1 percent, and we want athletes with less wear and tear on their bodies.

I'm not sure why it's gone in this direction. The kids are not driving it. Neither parents nor coaches are controlling the environment.

Do you recruit at tournaments?

Look, we've got people planning all these "events" with lots of teams playing lots of games. Coaches go to watch these events, so the organizers need kids to play on those teams. Parents get a group of kids to play. But then someone's daughter is the seventh player on the team and isn't getting enough time, so her mom or dad decides to start another team and get some other girls to play. And then it happens again, so you've got so many kids playing, it's watered down.

We're losing the value of sport—the value of losing and winning. Rewarding hard work is gone. It's about getting to play in college, so it's about a club team—not a sports team.

Have you been to any of the AAU games? Go watch a game. You'll see the parental environment. Parents allow those coaches to berate their kids, say and do anything—you'll hear some of the worst language ever. Anything goes because parents think it's going to help their kid get a scholarship. They hire "specialists" who say they can prepare their kid for college—both athletically and academically.

Here's the truth about scholarships: It's not my scholarship to give—it's the University of Richmond's scholarship. No high school or AAU coach is going to call a college coach and get a kid a scholarship. The only one who's going to get that kid a scholarship is that kid. And they have to be valuable to the specific university. We'll find the kids that are good enough.

I've found that generally, hard work yields positive results. But parents and kids equate time and money spent with value. A girl works harder in practice than current teammates—puts forth more effort than them running wind sprints. But there's no clock. She thinks she's working hard, but is she?

I don't want to hear a player spent three hours in the gym.

Why? Spend a good hard twenty minutes doing what you should be—length of time spent has allowed hard work to be excused away.

What other changes have you observed in your career?
All this time and money is spent in the name of improving our sport, but it's killing it, and it's not helping our kids. Even the recruiting process has been sped up. We used to sign kids in April of their senior year. Now it's November in their senior year. We used to only talk to seniors; now we can talk to juniors. There are some eighth and ninth graders who are signing letters of intent. They don't even understand what they are doing.

We, as a society, are putting kids in positions where they'll fail because they can't handle lack of success in the moment. We used to play to the highest person on a team; now it's the lowest because everyone wants to be happy. If kids are playing for their parents, it will catch up to them. Playing is a huge commitment. Many kids don't have that desire.

It's not easy playing at the college level, is it?
I tell recruits exactly what every day here will be like. It's going to start with classes, individual practices, a quick lunch, more classes, team practice, supper, studying, and bed. But when they get here, they seem surprised; they don't want it to be like that, and I wonder What didn't you get? I told you this is what it was going to be, and if you didn't want to do it, you should have said so back then.

The same thing happens in the classroom. They have to be good students. But even if they take college prep courses, they don't seem prepared to deal with harder classes. They get a bad grade; some kids fall apart when it happens.

Some of the parents don't realize till their kid's here, either—the hard work is just starting, not ending. And while they let AAU coaches treat their kids badly, they don't want the college coach to set the bar high—to expect their kid to work hard.

Parents have to let go or they're setting their kids up for failure. Sport needs to be fun.

The meaning of "team"

On September 20, 2019, the 1993 boys' basketball team was inducted into the Dodgeville High School Athletic Hall of Fame. We had not seen most of the boys—the men who were now in their early forties—for many years. Having recently written my own memories of their trip to State, I was eager to hear their reflections.

I listened carefully as Scott told me about the social time they spent together after the homecoming parade and the memories that bonded this team. When coach Chuck Tank asked them why they thought the team was so good, there was no hesitation.

Several responded: "We liked each other!"

I listened carefully the next day during the homecoming pep assembly where they were introduced. One of the players, who had played Division III basketball in college and became a teacher, coach, and superintendent, summarized their success and the basis of all successful teams: "We were a group of people who were all-in and had a shared vision."

And I listened carefully at the induction ceremony that evening as the men passed the microphone. I listened for the answer to how to brew the magic formula, how to orchestrate similar success. How can one achieve a winning season, a trip to State, and a lifetime of memories? The team members explained:

- They had a coach with a plan. The team had a goal. Someone's got to lead, and the team has to be on board.
- Several were natural athletes, and some had to work harder on their skills, but they all pushed themselves to become better and supported each other in the process.
- They were driven by the desire to be part of something bigger than themselves:

> "We liked each other."
> "We cared about each other."
> "We didn't care who scored; we just wanted to win."
> "We didn't want to let each other down."
> "I loved these guys and I still do."
> "We played for you—the community—we were representing our school; we were representing Dodgeville."

Like the teams Dad coached and Scott and I played on, this team was motivated by their relationships, by their respect for each other and for their coaches. Their skills complemented their teammates' and they supported each other because they each gave it their all.

It was a selfless endeavor—a true team effort.

And it happened before we forgot that the most rewarding magic is the kind the kids brew themselves.

Flagrant Fouls

Desire. Anticipation. Fun. The youth sports system has chipped away at the primary motivators and the most important outcome of playing. But it has also chipped away at the game itself. And the mental and physical well-being of children. If I were a referee, I would send the current youth sports system to the bench with five fouls.

First Foul: Loss of fundamentals

When more kids began playing more sports at all age levels, we needed more coaches. Parents volunteered. Some had valuable knowledge to share and worked well with young kids. Others were well-intentioned but didn't *know* fundamental skills, let alone how to *teach* them. And some took it all much too seriously, expecting elementary or middle-school kids to perform beyond their physical, mental, and emotional capabilities.

Based on the belief that playing games was the way to get better, local and traveling teams formed to supplement the high school schedule. Less time was spent on drills and practice, and seasons expanded to add more games to the schedules. All-day tournaments meant a team could play several games in one day. So kids got the experience of playing lots of games. Lots of games that provided lots of time to develop bad habits. By the time they got to play for their seventh-grade school team, a knowledgeable coach had to do a lot of work trying to undo bad habits already formed and had to explain to a parent that all the *hours* their child had spent playing did not make that child a great player.

In the mid-2010s I asked Dad what changes he had seen in high school basketball:

> *There was a huge difference between when I played and when your brothers played. The kids were a lot*

more talented than we were—at every grade level. They were also better coached at all schools. There was more knowledge of the game by then that was shared at coaching clinics, and more complex offenses and defenses.

But I started to see a big difference in skills in the 2000s. All of a sudden it seemed there were no good shooters. Maybe it's because kids spend more time on computers and video games—why practice shooting outside? There may be a few good ones, but I don't see the same abilities in shooting. It's a lost art because kids don't take the time to practice it.

About that same time Scott began working as an official for many middle school and junior varsity boys' and girls' basketball games. Most of the players had been playing since they were in elementary school, but it was on rare occasion that he encountered a team who had strong fundamentals and basketball sense. Fundamentals had declined. And so had sportsmanship.

Second Foul: Loss of respect for school teams, coaches, and referees

When Title IX ensured that girls would have opportunities to play sports, it ensured that, like the boys, girls could experience what it meant to be on a team. To learn that every member had a role. That each member was responsible for doing the best they could in that role by learning and developing their skills. That working together, a team was better than the sum of its parts. Lessons learned to carry us into adulthood and the workplace. There was pride in representing our school. The team came first. Members served the team.

But pay-to-play teams, for which the players and often the coach are handpicked, exist to serve the players. To be a showcase for their talents. Various levels of AAU teams exist to serve players of every skill level and parents of various income levels, especially those chasing a college scholarship. Don't like the coach? Not getting enough playing time? There's always another team you can play on.

When parents can find a club coach that says what they want to hear, it opens the door to abundant criticism of high school coaches. When we pay for something, its perceived value increases. If a kid is good enough to be a starter on her club team, why is she not starting on the school team?

And where does a player place her loyalty if she is instructed by different coaches with different philosophies about the same sport at the same time?

High school teacher-coaches are no longer the sole leaders of their team. They are under a great deal of pressure to balance the mission of high school sports with the outside pressures of club sports, parents, and other coaches. Many leave the role because of unrealistic expectations to produce a winning team. Some are dropping out because the year-round demands are too much to expect from their family and spouse. Others lose their jobs because school administrators bow to parents instead of backing the coach, the way Dad's superintendent did.

Applying the AAU mindset, if they don't get what they want, dissatisfied parents can move to another district, use open enrollment, or enroll in a private school in an effort to optimize their child's high school experience.

So much for school spirit and team loyalty.

Putting youth sports on a pedestal has also opened the door to bad behavior and poor sportsmanship by many coaches, players, and parents.

In the 1970s a parent who screamed at the ref from the bleachers was an embarrassment to his child and the other fans. A talented but cocky player didn't deserve respect. Coaches who began riding an official were quickly put in their place with a technical foul. And players who challenged an official found themselves sitting on the bench for the rest of the game and sometimes the next. Good or bad, sportsmanship reflected on a team and a community.

By the early to mid 2000s, thanks to all the hours they spent watching their children play, many parents believed that they knew the game as well as the coach, and the rules as well as the officials. And they became more vocal—berating players, coaches, and officials as though they were entitled for the price of admission. State high school sports associations implemented sportsmanship creeds to be read prior to every game.

Parents started coaching their children from the bleachers, making the coach's job even more difficult. Schools implemented codes of conduct for parents, as well as athletes, in an effort to remind parents that the game is not about them. They were advised about proper behavior when they attended games and had to be asked to refrain from gossip and derogatory social media posts.

I thought we couldn't fall any farther until in 2020 the Wisconsin State Legislature introduced a bipartisan bill that could fine unruly sports fans with up to a $10,000 fine and up to nine months in prison. They cited the increase in violent outbursts directed at officials and a National Association of Sports Officials survey report that 47 percent of sports officials have reported feeling unsafe and 13 percent had been physically assaulted by a fan.

In the fall of 2021, at halftime of local high school games, the announcer made a plea to respect the referees and explained the shortage of officials in our state, hoping to recruit people willing to do the job.

What will happen to high school sports when no one is willing to coach or referee?

Third Foul: Kids dropping out of sports

In 2003 a parenting columnist encouraged a writer whose nine-year-old daughter wanted to sign up for activities because her friends were doing it: "Don't feel guilty for having your daughter's best interests at heart. You be the parent and say 'no' to mind-boggling hectic schedules that tend to lead children to burn out as early as the seventh grade. In the end, less is more and more is less."

Two months later a *Wisconsin State Journal* article highlighted families who were committing enormous amounts of time and money to sports. The journalist demonstrated that the youth soccer world offered many families a sense of community and most parents were willing to make the sacrifice (and investment) because they were driven by wanting to do what's best for their children.

So, what is best for children?

Through the 2000s the tone of youth sports and parenting articles changed as parents began to feel the strain of the schedules and questioned the value of intense coaches and high-performance expectations at the elementary level. And some kids took themselves out of the game, doing for themselves what their parents couldn't. Barbara F. Meltz cited three pressure points of kids' sports in her article about burnout: social, physical, and parental. "When children feel these pressures," she wrote, "they get bored or unhappy and want to quit. That's not necessarily bad."

In 2020, according to the National Council of Youth Sports website, 70 percent of kids in sports quit by age thirteen. "They quit in part because they're not having fun, have ineffective coaches, overbearing parents or they can't afford to play."

Seventy percent of kids are quitting before the age I started to play.

There are many reasons to be concerned about the number of kids dropping out of sports, but it seems the reasons they do are staring us straight in the face. What is there to look forward to when they start so young? Are the kids who are enrolled to play just because they are a certain age really ready to play the game? Or are they there because it has become as routine to sign kids up for sports as to send them to school?

As just one example of how demands on kids' time have increased, when our daughters played and I coached City Rec basketball in the late 90s, it was for one hour on Saturday mornings for about eight to ten weeks. My current community offers youth basketball for girls in grades three to eight from October to February.

How many kids opt out of a sport because they've seen the excessive demands of playing year-round and the parental politics and don't want that to be part of their high school experience?

And how many are just worn out? By the time they get to high school, many kids are tired of sports, and they're just plain tired.

What started with good intentions has backfired. More is indeed less. With overbooked schedules and omnipresent technology, there is barely time for a child to think, let alone learn to figure out what's important to them.

In 2018 Dr. Michael Yogman, a Harvard Medical School pediatrician, advised in an *Atlanta Journal-Constitution* article, "This may seem old-fashioned, but there are skills to be learned when kids aren't told what to do." The headline of this news story was eerily familiar: "Doctor's orders: Let children just play."

Fourth Foul: Decline in learning life skills

I am saddened by what has happened to the game, but I am frightened by what is playing out in young adults. Age-appropriate and schedule-appropriate youth sports—and other extracurriculars—can help kids build confidence and resilience on their way to adulthood. But going back to the law of diminishing returns, we are in the zone where too much pizza (activity) and too much beer (parental involvement) have made us sick.

When parents began sitting in gym bleachers at all-day tournaments instead of watching their kids shoot hoops in the driveway, when they began coaching their children's teams and scheduling practices and meals, their children's activities became theirs. Instead of pursuing their own hobbies on the weekend or hosting other couples for a Saturday night of dinner and cards, they collapsed exhausted after a long day of travel and hours in the gym.

Soccer moms became helicopter parents. Helicopter parents became snowplow then bulldozer parents, determined to smooth the way for their child in sports and in life.

But children whose activities are micromanaged, whose parents resolve their problems, miss the window of opportunity to learn how to handle age-appropriate responsibilities and challenges. They miss a key lesson of growing up: learning they are capable. And they struggle as young adults.

My sister-in-law taught college students for over thirty years, but it was only in the last decade of her career in the 2010s that she had students challenge their grades, believing they should get an A for *doing* an assignment, not for doing it well.

College students of the past were responsible for knowing and completing degree requirements, for learning how to apply for financial aid, and how to navigate class registration. College freshmen of today want a checklist that tells them what to do, and digital badges for completion.

Students even struggle with how and when to study. My friend from college, dr. beth triplett, chief connector at leadership dots, shared her observations in this July 2019 blog post:

leadership dot #2601: tough love
by dr. beth triplett

I teach an accelerated version of an MBA class and in my last section students were lamenting at how challenged they were to complete the final paper on time. When I asked for feedback for the class, they suggested that I require an interim assignment where students had to provide their reference list in advance. (Presumably, this will provide an incentive for them to start working on their papers earlier in the course!)

They were quite vocal in their requests and even provided a well-thought-out rationale in writing after the class had ended—but I just couldn't bring myself to do it. It felt too much like coddling. If I try to teach anything in my courses it is relevant life lessons and requiring self-driven forethought and responsibility seemed to be good skills to reinforce (or learn?).

I worry that the bar for personal responsibility keeps getting pushed further and further into adulthood. It used to be that you had to take greater ownership for your actions as you grew as a child. Then it was when you entered high school. Then college was the mark of independence, only now life coaches are there to provide assistance in navigating the system. Are people now on their own when they begin their first job or are onboarding

buddies and mentors extending that phase of independence as well?...

Schools, sports and extracurricular activities
have resulted in very structured lives for our youth
and I see them challenged in transitioning to a
phase where they take responsibility for creating
their own schedules and deadlines. The tough love
on my syllabus may be the most valuable thing they
learn in class.

Out of the game with the fifth foul:
Youth sports injuries

No pain, no gain. Work through the pain. Be tough.

Those dated pieces of advice were not in the best interest
of high school athletes and are certainly not appropriate for
children whose muscles and bones are developing.

Physicians began sounding the alarm two decades ago as
they saw youth sports injuries increase in frequency and severity.
Overuse and chronic injuries have been recognized as a public
health issue. The Centers for Disease Control and Prevention
(CDC), the National Athletic Trainers Association (NATA), and
high school sports associations now dedicate time and effort to
educate coaches and parents about youth sports injuries.

According to the NATA website (in 2020), 90 percent
of kids will incur some sort of sports injury in their athletic
careers, 54 percent have played while injured, and 25 percent
of coaches and parents do nothing to prevent injuries.

Most of those childhood injuries will impact a child's sports experience; some will impact the rest of their life. Anyone who coaches or parents a child in sports has a responsibility to know the risks, provide age-appropriate activities, and advocate for athletic training services.

Can we change the narrative?

There are national youth sports organizations, as well as high school sports associations and local parks and recreation programs, working to address the problems and restore the benefits of youth sports. But it will take more parents to join the effort, to change society, to change the youth sports story.

To change the narrative it will take more parents to do what some friends of ours did in 2019. When they recognized the toll playing forty-five basketball games in a year was taking on their sixth-grade daughter, they made the decision for her to leave the team.

To change the narrative it will take more parents to acknowledge that it's not healthy for middle schoolers to go to school all day, then attend a team sport practice after school and another club sport practice or dance lessons that evening.

To change the narrative it will take more parents to delay their children's start in organized sports, to give their elementary-aged children time to play in the backyard, to read a book, to be bored, and to learn to entertain themselves.

It will take more parents who say enough is enough, this isn't how we want to raise our children.

As I finish writing in the spring of 2020, most activity has been cancelled, and we are staying home in an effort to slow the spread of the novel coronavirus (COVID-19). I can't help but wonder if some families are learning what they've been missing. I realize that having everyone at home every day and trying to balance work with facilitating online learning is more togetherness than any of us needs. But on my daily walks I have seen people doing things I haven't seen in years. A dad and his son playing catch with a football. A dad and two daughters shooting baskets in their driveway. Sisters rollerblading on the sidewalk. Entire families taking an evening walk together. Parents spending time with their children in a way that isn't possible when schedules are jammed with activities that require travel and days spent in gyms.

I wonder if this ordeal will help some parents redefine what it means to win. Maybe they will take the time to evaluate the options and choose what is truly best for their children. Maybe instead of returning to frantic, jam-packed schedules, they'll choose to scale back to a more kid- and-family-friendly pace of life.

For parents who want to call time-out and make some changes, I offer three pieces of advice:

Distinguish your desire from your child's

Dan Shanoff shared his own "aha moment" in his 2016 story "Time to give my son the keys to his own sports journey." After dropping his ten-year-old off at a prestigious school's basketball camp, he felt more ashamed of himself than excited for his son. He admitted attending the camp was something *he* wanted. And he realized his son would enjoy his sports experience a whole lot more if it was driven by his own desire. And ultimately, Dan would too.

If your children are in elementary school, watch their interests carefully, and let them choose one or two activities that bring them joy *this year.* Accept that they are learning about themselves and next year they may choose something else. Introduce kids to sports in an age-appropriate way: *when they express an interest.* Unless they are truly a sports prodigy, expecting children to develop skills before their body is ready will lead to frustration at best, injury at worst. Consider a one-sport-per-season rule for your kids.

If your child is an overbooked middle-schooler, take some time to really watch as they play or perform. Do you see joy on their face? Have a heart-to-heart talk to help them (or you) understand what activities make them happy. Give them permission to drop out if they participate in an extracurricular solely to please someone else. Help them find something that is a better fit.

If your child is in high school, they may truly enjoy sports and activities, they may be burned out and looking for a way out, or they may have already abandoned some activities that kept them busy for years. Graduation is on the horizon but there is still time to make sure they have some life skills, like running a clothes washer, managing money, and scheduling a doctor's appointment. Can they make a meal? Do they know how to persevere on a long-term project? If they dropped sports, could they get a part-time job?

I recently met the mother of an eighteen-month-old who was concerned about whether and when to have her child participate in sports. She felt pressured by the toddler-parent programs to introduce children to sport, but the idea didn't sit well with her. Her concerns reminded me of my fear that children were learning math skills in daycare while I danced in the living room with my preschoolers.

Do you have a friend who feels the same way about over-booked kids? More than one friend? Friends who have other friends? Form a supportive parenting team. Change FOMO (fear of missing out) to JOMO (joy of missing out) and become the cool parents whose kids build forts in the backyard and play hide-and-go-seek till dusk.

Trust your intuition. Do what is truly best for each of your children and your family.

Be honest with yourself about what you want your child to gain from sport

People used to say that playing sports was good for kids because it provided leadership skills necessary in the work world. Because they could learn how to work hard and bounce back from defeat. Because they could learn what teamwork is all about. And they could learn all that while having fun.

I'm not sure how many people still say that. And I'm not sure how much of it is still true. But I am hopeful because I think there are parents who still want their children to learn those values from sport. Even if a minority continues to seek something else.

In the book *The Matheny Manifesto*, former Major League Baseball player and St. Louis Cardinals Manager Mike Matheny shares his experience of coaching his ten-year-old son's baseball team. He knew what he would be dealing with when a group of parents asked him to coach. He agreed and held a meeting with the parents to make it very clear that he was in charge. He laid out his approach, expectations, and philosophy in a letter he read to the group. His main goals were to:

- Teach the boys the right way to play baseball
- Make a positive impact on them as young men
- Do it with class

He explained that parents need to be silent sources of encouragement. That umpires would be respected. That he would teach the boys how to think about the game as they played it. That the boys could learn and play in several positions, but ultimately the coaches would place them in the position where they could most help the team. The team would not travel because there was plenty of local competition. The boys would be expected to hustle, always thinking about the game and what they could do to help the team.

Mike Matheny knew his system would work because it was how he learned the game. He wasn't coaching to create college or professional players. He was coaching to instill values in the boys they could apply in their workplaces, homes and families, and communities someday.

Believe it or not, a few parents passed on this opportunity. I'm sure the children who played for Coach Matheny will never forget the lessons they learned.

*

In Minnesota, after reading Joe Ehrmann's book *InSideOut Coaching: How Sports Can Transform Lives*, a group of administrators realized their coaches were set up to fail because the goal of sport had overshadowed its purpose. Recognizing that 97 percent of high school athletes do not go on to play collegiate sports, in 2013 the Minnesota State High School League started a program called WHY WE PLAY and began training high school athletic administrators and coaches on the purpose of education-based athletics. Associate Director Jody Redman explained, "The goal is to win, and coaches should be playing and planning and preparing to win the game but that's not the purpose. The purpose is the human growth and development of kids through their sports experience and connecting them to caring adults in their learning communities so they can also have academic success."

*

Not everyone has a Mike Matheny living in their neighborhood. And maybe your state high school sports association or local school district has been slow to refocus the purpose of school sports. But every sports parent can take responsibility for their role in shaping their child's experience. If you aren't sure where to start, John M. Tauer's book, *Why Less is More for WOSPs (Well-Intentioned, Overinvolved Sports Parents): How to be the best Sports Parent you can be*, can be a great guide. A coach and researcher, Tauer explores the questions and problems of youth sports and offers suggestions for parents to encourage a good experience for their children and themselves.

There are national organizations like the Women's Sports Foundation that work for equity in youth sports so all kids can have the opportunity to play regardless of income, promote age-appropriate sports, and encourage good sportsmanship on the part of players and parents.

But what really matters is what is happening in your own community, in your own school district. Are the administrators of youth sports focused on the purpose? More importantly, as a parent, are you? Groups of like-minded people are what changed youth sports to what it is today, and what can change it again.

Maybe you're the one who needs to start the conversation in your town or school district. Others will be relieved to join you. Dial the number of games back a few notches. Insist on sports schedules that don't overlap and include a week or two break in-between so kids can get excited about the next offering. Focus on fun and teach sports at age-appropriate levels.

Working with other families you can bring about change. Change that allows kids the chance to gain the traditional benefits of sport. The chance to have fun.

Don't play not to lose. Play to win.

Let them play safe

Last, but certainly not least: learn about youth sports injuries. Do your children's coaches practice age-appropriate skills? Are they trained in injury prevention best practices? What is the philosophy of your recreation league? Your school district? Are athletic trainers available to guide coaches and players on injury prevention as well as to evaluate and treat injuries?

A couple quick Google searches will produce hundreds of articles about youth sports injuries. How they happen. How they are treated. And how they can be prevented. Every sports parent should take the time to learn enough to make good choices for their child. Explore the National Athletic Trainers Association website. Learn what your local health care provider offers in injury prevention programs. And check out other resources at the back of this book.

Because the last thing you want to hear is, "Mom, I hurt my knee."

FINAL BUZZER

April 27, 2018

Sitting graveside at the cemetery, my mind drifted from the priest's message to Dad's last evening with us. His health had declined rapidly over a few days, but I did not recognize his delirious request as a signal that he wanted to call a final timeout.

"I need a whistle! Get me a whistle!"

"Dad, what do you need a whistle for?"

"I need to get people's attention. I have something to say."

"I'm sorry . . . we don't have a whistle, Dad."

I urged him to listen to the Cubs game playing on the bedside radio.

The next morning he was gone.

I turned to see the tombstone with the etched basketball next to his name.

"Not because I was a great player. I wasn't. But because the game did so much for me in life."

*

Basketball had a significant impact on everyone in our family. None of us were great players. We didn't win any state championships. And not one of us got a college scholarship. We got a whole lot more.

ACKNOWLEDGEMENTS

Many thanks to my editors. Christine Keleny of CKBooks Publishing challenged me to focus on my book's purpose and reorganize my first draft. Lillian Duggan of The Ideal Word helped me fine-tune the final manuscript with her thoughtful review, and she found the errors I couldn't see after ten years of reading my own writing. Everyone needs an editor—or two!

Great appreciation to my early readers who offered encouragement and feedback on first drafts: Greg Alleman, Jennifer Bradley, Holli Dietrick, Eric Miller, and Deborah Yenser; to Jennifer Bradley, Eric Miller, and Orsolya Szecsi for their marketing expertise.

Love and hugs to my sister-in-law, Diane Sandage, for reviewing the first printed book and to my daughter, Kylee Hawkinson, for designing the book cover and my website.

Lifelong gratitude to my high school English teachers Margaret Miller, Larry Nelson, and Jerilyn Strohecker for setting high expectations and encouraging my interest in reading and writing.

Friendship and special thanks to my Lena-Winslow Girls'

Basketball teammates for being such an important part of my life. We made history together. And though our coach, Marvin Kaiser, passed in 2019, he should never be forgotten for starting our high school girls' basketball program.

Love to my dear writer-friends, who have supported me at different stages of this endeavor, and my life: Greer Deneen, Eileen Frank, Denise LaBudda, and Nicole Miller.

Finally, without my parents, Richard and Mary Maher; my brothers, Patrick, Daniel, and Michael; my husband Scott and daughters Lauren and Kylee, there would be no story. Thank you for being my family. I love you all.

ABOUT THE AUTHOR

Photo credit: Paul L. Newby II

Christine (Maher) Hawkinson began writing poems at the age of seven and still has the notebook her mother purchased specifically for her creations. Growing up, she spent more time reading than playing backyard games, and more time watching other people play sports than playing them herself.

After graduating with a marketing degree from Western Illinois University, she discovered early in her career it was writing newsletters that she enjoyed most. Twenty years later, she earned a Master of Science in Family and Consumer Journalism from the University of Wisconsin–Madison.

Writing her thesis, "Let Them Play Safe: A Qualitative

Analysis of Coaches' and Athletic Directors' Stance on Injury Prevention," fueled her interest in youth sports culture. When her youngest daughter left for college, she began writing *50 Years in the Bleachers*. Time and distance allowed her to reflect on the evolution of youth sports. Desire, discipline, and structure kept her on task as she wrote her book over ten years, mostly one hour at a time.

Hawkinson has worked for private and public organizations in a variety of writing roles and is currently a senior communications writer for the University of Wisconsin–Madison. Her most rewarding experiences have been helping her husband raise two wonderful daughters and writing *50 Years in the Bleachers*.

She lives with her husband in Prairie du Sac, WI. When not at her writing desk, she enjoys listening to live local music, riding her bike on the Great Sauk State Trail, and watching for eagles as she walks near the Wisconsin River. She keeps a journal of ideas for writing projects and is always looking for her next adventure.

Learn more at
christinehawkinson.com
ChristineHawkinsonWrites

RESOURCES

Here are a few of the organizations working to reinvent youth sports or prevent injuries. Learn about others on my website, *https://www.christinehawkinson.com,* or by subscribing to my blog, *Lessons from the driveway,* at https://www.christinehawkinson.com/blog.

The Aspen Institute – Project Play
   https://www.aspenprojectplay.org

At Your Own Risk – A Safer Approach to Work, Life and Sport
   https://www.atyourownrisk.org/youth-sports

Center for Disease Control and Prevention (CDC) HEADS UP to Youth Sports
   https://www.cdc.gov/headsup/youthsports/index.html

Change It Up – Playing Different Sports Is Better for Our Kids
   https://playmoresports.activeforlife.com

InSideOut Initiative
https://insideoutinitiative.org

Johns Hopkins All Children's Hospital
https://www.hopkinsallchildrens.org/Services/
Pediatric-Sports-Medicine

National Athletic Trainers Association – Youth Sports Safety
https://www.nata.org/advocacy/youth-sports-safety

Positive Coaching Alliance
https://positivecoach.org/

TrueSport
https://truesport.org/

Women's Sports Foundation
https://www.womenssportsfoundation.org

BIBLIOGRAPHY

Bigelow, Bob, Tom Moroney, and Linda Hall. *Just Let the Kids Play: How to Stop Other Adults from Ruining Your Child's Fun and Success in Youth Sports.* Deerfield Beach, Florida: Health Communications, Inc., 2001.

Cohen, Kelly. "Kids aren't playing enough sports. The culprit? Cost." ESPN, August 11, 2019. https://www.espn.com/espn/story/_/id/27356477/kids-playing-enough-sports-culprit-cost.

Cooky, Cheryl, Michael A. Messner, and Michela Musto. "'It's dude time!': A Quarter Century of Excluding Women's Sports in Televised News and Highlight Shows." *Communication & Sport*, 3, 3 (2015): 261–287.

Das, Andrew. "U.S. Women's Soccer Team Sues U.S. Soccer for Gender Discrimination." *New York Times*, March 8, 2019.

DeBoer, Kathleen J. *Gender and Competition: How Men and Women Approach Work and Play Differently.* Coach's Choice, 2004.

Dickey, Jack. "In the Fight for Women's Equality, Muffet McGraw Finds Her Moment." *Sports Illustrated*, June 17, 2019.

Gregory, Sean. "How Kids' Sports Became a $15 Billion Industry." *Time*, August 24, 2017.

Griggs, Brandon. "You may not know her name. But Bernice Sandler, 'Godmother of Title IX,' changed women's rights forever." CNN, January 13, 2019. https://www.cnn.com/2019/01/08/us/bernice-sandler-title-ix-dies/index.html.

Healy, Melissa. "Doctor's orders: Let children just play." *Los Angeles Times*, September 14, 2018.

Lane Tech College Prep High School. "History." *http://www.lanetech.org/about/history.*

Libit, Daniel. "Soccer can be engine that drives a family." *Wisconsin State Journal*, July 20, 2003.

Lueneburg, Chris. "WIAA to parents: 'Cool it." Channel3000, January 11, 2019. https://www.channel3000.com/wiaa-to-parents-cool-it.

Matheny, Mike with Jerry B. Jenkins, *The Matheny Manifesto: A Young Manager's Old-School Views on Success in Sports and Life.* New York: Crown Archetype, 2015.

McLean, Trevor. "What is AAU Basketball (Including Pros and Cons)?" (blog post). Basketball for Coaches. https://www.basketballforcoaches.com/what-is-aau-basketball/.

Meltz, Barbara F. "Right attitude keeps kids from burning out on sports." *Boston Globe* (in *Wisconsin State Journal*), 2003.

National Athletic Trainers Association. https://www.nata.org/.

National Collegiate Athletic Association. "Estimated probability of competing in college athletics." *https://www.ncaa.org/about/resources/research/estimated-probability-competing-college-athletics.*.

National Council of Youth Sports. https://www.ncys.org.

Parent to Parent column, *Limit children's activities*, Wisconsin State Journal, May 11, 2003.

Plaschke, Bill. "I regret marginalizing Pat Summitt's greatness." *Los Angeles Times*, June 28, 2016. https://www.latimes.com/sports/nba/la-sp-pat-summitt-plaschke-20160628-snap-story.html.

Porter, Cody. "Minnesota's WHY WE PLAY Initiative Teaches Purpose of Educational Sports." National Federation of State High School Associations, February 8, 2016. https://www.nfhs.org/articles/minnesota-s-why-we-play-initiative-teaches-purpose-of-educational-sports.

Shanoff, Dan. "Time to give my son the keys to his own sports journey." ESPN Voices, July 13, 2016. https://www.espn.com/espnw/voices/story/_/id/17049390/time-give-my-son-keys-own-sports-journey.

Tauer, John M., PhD. *Why Less Is More for WOSPs (Well-Intentioned, Overinvolved Sports Parents): How to be the best sports parent you can be.* Saint Paul, Minnesota: Beaver's Pond Press, 2015.

triplett, beth. "leadership dot #2601: tough love." leadership dots, July 30, 2019. *https://leadershipdots.com/2019/07/30/leadership-dot-2601-tough-love.*

Wiseman, Rosalind. *Queen Bees & Wannabes: Helping Your Daughter Survive Cliques, Gossip, Boyfriends, and Other Realities of Adolescence.* New York: Crown, 2002.

Additional inspiration provided by

Asquith, Christina. "Sue the Coach! Want to get your kid more playing time? Hate the varsity's game plan? Just call your lawyer." Scorecard, November 11, 2002.

Ehrmann, Joe. *InSideOut Coaching: How Sports Can Transform Lives.* New York: Simon & Schuster, 2011.

Galloway, Jason. "North Crawford School District faces potential lawsuit over players' all-conference snub." *Wisconsin State Journal, May 8, 2014.*

Hernandez, Ron. "Parents ought to be cognizant of 'Crossing the Line.'" *Wisconsin State Journal*, August 27, 2002.

Hernandez, Ron. "Participation decline merits full-court press." *Wisconsin State Journal*, November 13, 2012.

Hernandez, Ron. "Will clubs hurt soccer in schools?" *Wisconsin State Journal*, April 22, 2003.

Oates, Tom. "Meddling parents ruin coaching." *Wisconsin State Journal*, June 23, 2003.

Reddy, Sumathi. "The Rise of Overuse Injuries in Youth Baseball." *Wall Street Journal*, June 6, 2016.

Svokos, Alexandra. "A Majority of High Schools Lack Full-Time Athletic Trainers to Keep Kids Safe." Huffpost, December 6, 2017.

CPSIA information can be obtained
at www.ICGtesting.com
Printed in the USA
LVHW100953151122
733200LV00010B/78

9 798985 234800